Ga

P

GW00601024

Crazy Gary's Mobile
> **The Drowned World, Fags**
> **Cancer Time**

Crazy Gary's Mobile Disco: 'Immaculately written . . . a roaring monster of a play.' *Tribune*

The Shadow of a Boy: 'A beautiful, critical, generous play.' *Sunday Times*

The Drowned World: 'Startlingly confident . . . linguistically daring, conceptually mesmerising.' *Evening Standard*

Fags: A companion piece to *Cancer Time*, first produced in 2001.

Cancer Time: 'An accomplished play that works cleverly against your expectations.' *Time Out*

Gary Owen went to school in Bridgend and then studied at Sidney Sussex College, Cambridge, and at the European Film College in Denmark. Formerly a script editor for BBC Wales Drama, his plays are *Crazy Gary's Mobile Disco* (Paines Plough and Sgript Cymru, 2001), *The Shadow of a Boy* (National Theatre, 2002), *The Drowned World* (Paines Plough, 2002), *Fags* (Slush Theatre, Aberystwyth Arts Centre, 2001), *Amser Canser* (Royal Welsh College of Music and Drama, 2003), *Cancer Time* – an English Language version of *Amser Canser* – (Theatre 503 Latchmere, London, 2004), and *Ghost City* (Sgript Cymru, 2004). *The Shadow of a Boy* was joint winner of the 2002 George Devine Award and winner of the 2003 Meyer Whitworth Award. *The Drowned World* won a Fringe First at the Edinburgh Festival 2002, and was joint winner of the 2003 Pearson Best Play Award. For young people he has written *The Green* for the National Theatre's Assembly Project, and *SK8*, a hip-hop musical for the Theatre Royal, Plymouth.

by the same author and available from Methuen Drama

Ghost City

GARY OWEN

Plays: 1

Crazy Gary's Mobile Disco
The Shadow of a Boy
The Drowned World
Fags
Cancer Time

with an introduction by Vicky Featherstone

Methuen Drama

Published by Methuen Drama

First published in 2005 by
Methuen Publishing Limited
Methuen Drama
A and C Black Publishers Limited
36 Soho Square
London W1D 3QY

www.methuendrama.com

Cover image: Llyn Celyn Reservoir, North Wales. In 1965, amidst much protest, the rural Welsh village of Capel Celyn was submerged beneath the Tryweryn Reservoir to supply the borough of Liverpool with water.

A CIP catalogue record for this book is available from the British Library

ISBN 978 0 413 77481 1

Available in the USA from Bloomsbury Academic & Professional,
175 Fifth Avenue/3rd Floor, New York, NY 10010
www.BloomsburyAcademicUSA.com

Typeset by SX Composing DTP, Rayleigh, Essex
Printed and bound in Great Britain by
CPI Antony Rowe, Chippenham and Eastbourne

Contents

Gary Owen:
A Chronology

2001   *Crazy Gary's Mobile Disco* (Paines Plough and Sgript
       Cymru, Chapter Arts Centre, Cardiff)
       Fags (Slush Theatre, Aberystwyth Arts Centre)

2002   *The Shadow of a Boy* (Loft, National Theatre). Joint
       winner of the George Devine Award and winner of
       the Meyer Whitworth Award.
       The Drowned World (Paines Plough, Traverse Theatre,
       Edinburgh). Winner of an Edinburgh Fringe First
       and joint winner of the Pearson Best Play Award.

2003   *Amser Canser* (Royal Welsh College of Music &
       Drama)
       SK8 (Young Company, The Drum, Plymouth)

2004   *Ghost City* (Sgript Cymru, Chapter Arts, Cardiff)
       Cancer Time (Theatre 503 & Caird Company,
       Theatre 503, London)

Introduction

A volume of plays is a hugely prestigious and important moment in a playwright's career, giving deserved place for recognition and reflection. It is testament to Gary Owen's hunger for the theatre and his ability to illuminate our existence that there are five plays which are worthy of a volume in such a short space of time.

For it was only spring 1999 when *Crazy Gary's Mobile Disco* arrived at Paines Plough – by default, having been regretfully rejected by the Traverse in Edinburgh. Regretfully, in that with a Scottish remit they were unable to produce what was clearly a star (even a Welsh one) in the ascendant. Luckily they sent it to me. It is the only play I have ever read and committed to produce without meeting the writer. Gary was not a frequent theatre-goer and was rightly proud not to share a 'London-based new-writing' frame of reference for his work. Our first brief and quite painful meeting involved a shocked Gary, staring at us wildly, not really believing that the play he had written some time earlier, as three monologues for his actor friends to use as audition speeches, was going to be produced.

What struck me immediately when I read *Crazy Gary* was the force of the language and the dynamism with which I was drawn in to the world of the play. This was coupled with an overwhelming disappointment that this writer who had come so highly recommended was just another one of the school of 'boys' writing' which was so prevalent: a bit of swearing, a night out well recounted – all considered stuff enough for contemporary drama. But I read on. And a transformation took place. That was of course what Gary had wanted us to think.

I was drawn into a dark world of survival of the fittest, of the nihilistic no-hope land of small-town Britain and what ultimately is a piece about the beauty of retribution and our endless optimism about the possibility of being saved. The storytelling is so complex and cunningly crafted that as you move through the play every possible connection or cause and effect is thoroughly mined. It is also in places mind-

numbingly funny. In the form of monologue we only ever
have the characters' word for it, yet Gary creates a picture
of a small town in Wales which is brutal, complete, and
peopled by many sorts. At its heart is violence, whether in
the past, as we learn how the three boys are linked, or in the
present – in order to survive, either with Mathew Melody
killing ga-ga Tesco lady's cat or with Russell finally killing
Crazy Gary. But place this violence and brutality against the
sophistication of language structure and a rhythm of
dialogue which is almost mathematical and therefore
musical, and it is beguiling, stimulating and enthralling. It is
very much an emotional, romantic tale about escaping your
lot and your right to do so.

Throughout the process of casting, script development
and indeed rehearsal, Gary appeared constantly displeased,
so much so that I seriously began to wonder if I could ever
do justice to such a righteous writer with such high ideals.
But he also seemed to care about us all so much. The
paradox was one which all at Paines Plough fell in love with
and which set me a great challenge. I really wanted to
please him.

When Gary asked me to read the first draft of *The Shadow
of a Boy*, I began to notice something about his writing. Fear.
Both a fear for the here and now, but also a nostalgic
throwback to the awful moment in your life when you
realise you have absolutely no control over your destiny. We
are at the mercy of those who are in charge of the
apocalypse at whatever level that is, and *The Shadow of a Boy*
throws all of those at Luke: the death of parents, nuclear
threat, sexual awakening and going up to big school. How
are we able to grow into rounded and mature adults when
we have to deal with such ordeals as a child? It is so different
from *Crazy Gary*, not only proving the monologue cynics
wrong, that yes he can write dialogue, but also revealing
more of the charm and care that is part of his storytelling.
That Gary had his debut at the National Theatre with what
was only his second play was well deserved.

Some time later that year, Gary arrived at my office with
the first draft of his next commission for Paines Plough. It

was *The Drowned World*. The experience of developing that play, seeking to understand it on any level and put it before an audience, is one from which I learnt so much. Luckily I was able to get two stabs at it as it had a second run after its initial Edinburgh opening, in January of 2003 at the Bush Theatre in London. Working with the same cast on the second run, we were immediately embarrassed by how little we had understood it. This to me is always exciting, particularly when something has been well received. It proves it is a great piece of work. The genesis of the play always thrilled me and I felt it was a channelling of many experiences and observations that brought it into being. There was, for example, Gary's own experience at Cambridge as the clever working-class kid who had got in, but never felt accepted. (And who obviously thought all the well-bred girls had a certain beauty about them even though they made him feel less of himself, not more.) Coupled with this experience was the observation that there was a covetousness of the actual body from those who were ethnically cleansing their fellow humans.

Before this time, Gary had started going to the theatre in earnest and, without being patronising to him, realised that plays did not need to be about the world in which you actually lived. Metaphor could speak louder and more effectively, especially if what you wanted to say or what you observed was politically colossal and hard to understand.

The play is another example of masterful, apparently seamless storytelling, which shocks and reviles us with the need and brutality at its core. But it shares the same need for salvation shown in *Crazy Gary* and the same fear of apocalypse in *The Shadow of a Boy*. The central image of a world which is drowned in order to attempt renewal, yet repeats the same mistakes again, is heart-breaking.

In the dress rehearsal at the Bush, at the moment when Julian rushes out of the cellar into the sunshine and is kicked to death, Gary ran out of the theatre. I read this as being overwhelmed by the power of what we were creating. Not so. Gary had finally realised what that bit meant and it was the opposite of our triumphant and celebratory escape. *The*

Drowned World defies much explanation – it is a great play that is visionary in its perception and terrifying in its vision. I enjoy having it in my head.

> . . . And I don't feel
> There is any place for sentimentality,
> Not in a truly modern Britain living under
> The constant threat of apocalyptic terrorism.

When I was re-reading the five plays which are published here, these words spoken by Mared in *Cancer Time* really leapt out at me, highlighting a recurring idea in Gary's work: the desperately beating heart of the ordinary trying to survive the horror that our world imposes upon it. It is from everywhere normal and known that the material springs, yet it is in that horror that it becomes dramatic, urgent and political. It is with the articulate yet disenfranchised among us that Gary deals, and the originality and clarity with which he does so continues to astound me. In a way, Gary's work is my ideal. It is a poetic, strongly linguistic voice which is fearless of enormous ideas, complex and deeply layered, but which starts from a personal and often tender place. From there it moves us through fear and pain with wit and cruelty whilst somewhere in there, for those of us who need to see it, is the light of redemption. What a package. Sometimes it is more complete than others, but it is always ambitious and challenging, transforming and surprising.

Cancer Time was written in Welsh, to be performed in Welsh. It must not be forgotten that Gary is a bilingual writer and engages entirely with all the positive and negative of this. He applauds the Welsh language while also suggesting the following:

> … If we didn't have this
> Half-rotted language to prop up, the Welsh nation'd be
> Bestriding the world like a fuckin cultural colossus by
now.

Gary Owen at his confrontational, poetic and complex best. A playwright whose very pulse beats with the knowledge of what a shitty place the world can be, but who chooses always to examine it through the most humane, ordinary and fearful characters. There is huge moral judgement in Gary's work, but exacted with such skill and in such a vital context that it is not the simplicity of characters good and bad with which we are dealing, rather a detailed and layered set of circumstances which facilitate our understanding of action, survival and means of escape.

When Gary asked if he could write a piece for our Wild Lunch season, I was surprised. *Fags* has the same character as the more transgressive *Cancer Time*, but is about the simplest of things, a grown-up and very differently educated child's frustration with his mother smoking. It is very funny, beautiful and full of sentiment. I found it intensely pleasing that Gary also felt theatre was for the apparently tiny, the personal and the deeply-felt. It proved to me that here is a writer for whom theatre really is his form – a place to experiment with anything you want to say, in any way you believe you should. The drive behind this assures me that it will not be long before we are looking at a *Plays 2*. I hope so, because the world does not become a better place to live – just increasingly complex. For me, it is only with the vision and voice of playwrights like Gary that we can ever attempt to order it and maybe transcend it. His plays do not solve anything, but give us a way to think about things which is more healthy than 24-hour news bulletins or endless opinion pieces in the broadsheets.

To meet someone in the raw and open moment of their emerging talent is one of the true joys of what I do. It is an event to encounter true thinking, true reflection and the desire to order this into something for public consumption. I am more than fortunate to work with such people.

Yes, a volume is a great thing; but don't reflect, Gary, don't stop for a moment.

Vicky Featherstone
2005

Crazy Gary's Mobile Disco

diolch: Carole Byrne Jones, Andrea Smith, John Hefin, Gala Antipenko, Joachim Trier, Christina Rosendahl, Rob Storr, James Topping, Craig Russell, Angharad Herbert, Gilly Adams, Winsome Pinnock, Pedr James, Maggie Russell, Michael McCoy, Jessica Dromgoole, Vicky Featherstone and all my family.

for: all the weapons-grade honeys who've been inappropriately handled, 1989–2001: you can take this as one great big hey look I'm really really sorry.

Crazy Gary's Mobile Disco was first performed at Chapter Arts Centre, Cardiff, on 8 February 2001. The cast was as follows:

Gary	David Rees Talbot
Mathew D. Melody	Steven Meo
Russell Markham	Richard Mylan

Directed by Vicky Featherstone
Designed by Georgia Sion
Lighting by Natasha Chivers

1: booty call

Right. Fuck it. I'm gonna fucking spoil it for you all. I'm
gonna tell you how this story ends right now.

When I was growing up there was all this – nuclear
paranoia shit. All this – 'If the air-raid warning came what
would you do, if you only had three minutes to live?'

If I only had three minutes left to live, I'd carry on just as I
am. Because in three minutes' time, I'm gonna be fucking
. . . in heaven.

I'm gonna be fucking the fittest chick in the whole wide
bastard world.

So sod all that 'will he get her, won't he get her' bullshit –
I'm telling you now, this all ends with me pulling the perfect
girl.

Thursday night is disco night down the Boar's Head. My
disco night. Every fucker knows that. Every fucker, it seems,
except Brian the bitch of a landlord, who has decided to
replace the disco with . . . kara-fuckin-oke. Kara-fuckin-oke
run by a ginger-haired twat with big red plastic glasses and a
big floppy red bow-tie.

I cannot; I will not allow my people to suffer like this.

I take my place at the crowded bar, and wait.

Beat.

Three songs in, the moment presents itself – the karaoke
twat slips off to the toilet.

I down my pint.

The karaoke gimp is there at the left-hand stall. He senses
me coming in, and flicks his head round to look at me. I
walk towards the sinks and I stop, for the slightest hint of a
second, right behind him. I don't really stop, I just . . . pause
for a tiny half a heartbeat behind him where he can't see

me. And the trickle of his piss against the porcelain comes to a stop as he clenches up in fear.

I head on towards the sink, like I'm going to wash my hands. His gaze is fixed dead ahead but his whole attention is focused on me. He stands there, at once shitting himself, and yet, at the same time, cruelly unable to piss.

I rinse my hands under the taps and – it all comes together for me. From the bar I can still hear the chords from his karaoke machine, and I just . . . hum along to them –

He hums 'You've Lost That Loving Feeling'.

'If you feel like a sing-song, you should have a go,' he says.

I stop what I'm doing. I stop with the rinsing my hands under the taps and slowly, slowly turn my head round to look at him.

'Did you just say things to me?' I ask him.

He stands there, grinning desperately. 'I just meant –' he starts, but I'm on my run now and he's not stopping me.

'Did you just say things to me in the *gents* for fuck's sake?'

'I didn't mean anything by it –'

'Jesus Christ,' I say, 'what the fuck is the world coming to? Fucking gaylords trying it on in the gents of my own bastard local, for fuck's sake.'

'Oh . . . ' he goes, 'oh no, I wasn't trying it on, I'm not a gaylord –'

'Well, you obviously fucking are,' I say. He doesn't know quite how to come back to that. So he just says, 'I'm not.'

'No?'

'No,' he goes.

'Well, in that case,' I go, 'how the *fuck* do you explain that?' And I jab at his great big poofy red fucking bow-tie, ' 'Cause that is just about as gay as you can get.'

'Oh,' he says, with this great big surge of relief, 'that's just my costume. I do the karaoke, see. I'm the karaoke bloke.'

'Right,' I say. 'Right. So tell me, karaoke bloke – what the fuck're you doing here then?'

You can see then, in his eyes, you can see it just beginning to occur to him that there's more going on here than he thought. More, and worse.

'Well, I'm doing the karaoke, aren't I. Here. Tonight.'

'No you're fucking not,' I say.

'Well . . . I am,' he goes.

'No you fucking can't be,' I say, ''cause tonight is Thursday night, and Thursday night, as every fucker knows, is disco night. *My* disco night.'

Beat.

'Oh,' he says, 'you're the disco guy, are you?'

'That is abso-fuckin-lutely what am I,' I tell him.

'Right,' he says, 'well,' and he takes off his stupid big glasses and inspects them for muck. 'Thing is, mate, it's not up to me, is it? I mean . . . ' and he shrugs like he's letting me in on some super-fucking-obvious fact of life which I am just too retarded to get a grip on, 'if you lose the crowd, you're gonna lose the gig, aren't you?'

He stands there polishing his glasses and shrugging at me. With this look like – here we are, businessmen having a business discussion and it just so happens that he's in the superior position and what can you do about it.

And what I do about it is: I let him get on with it. I let him imagine he can look down on me. I let him pour it out, and I eat it all up. I let all that shit come and settle in my belly.

And so he puts his glasses back on and straightens his jacket and even extends his hand towards me, and says 'No hard feelings then?'

I step towards him.

And I reach out, like I'm reaching for his hand, and then I grab his head, I grab a handful of his hair, and I slam his face down into the porcelain, so hard that it bangs and bounces straight off, so fast that his head is back where it started before he even realises what's happened, and the only evidence that anything has happened is the sudden burning sensation in his forehead and the absence of his glasses, which have fallen off his face into the sink.

'What did you do that for?' he goes, scrabbling around for his specs.

'You are fuckin with my disco,' I tell him. 'Anyone who fucks with my disco, dies.'

The karaoke twat backs into the corner, blinking and making this little mewling noise. I go after him.

'Do your eyes give you trouble?' I ask him. 'Do you find short-sightedness is a problem for you?

'I can bring all that to an end for you,' I tell him. 'Poor sight need never trouble you again.'

He folds up, sinks down on to the floor and hugs himself, eyes closed and shaking and he just whispers, 'Please don't. Please don't. Please don't . . . '

Beat.

I have to leave at that point. 'Cause he does this thing. This thing which means that either I have to just leave, or I have to –

I'm not even back at the bar when the plug gets pulled on the outro of the classic sixties ballad.

I kick off another pint, and watch the karaoke twat as he dismantles his equipment and scuttles off, never daring to meet my eye.

So it's mission totally accomplished. Thursday nights at the Boar's Head are mine again.

But – just to my left, just next to me at the bar, there is a spoddy little bastard, and he is ill-advisedly allowing his elbow to knock against mine as he struggles to attract the attention of the bar staff. He's stuck – he's got the bar presence of a fucking . . .

Pauses to consider.

. . . twat, and he's starting to sweat it that he's never going to get served, so he's half-pretending that he's not really trying to, half-carrying on his conversation, 'Well, you see, Miranda, I think when you're brought up in cramped streets and beneath close horizons, it just *is* going to foster a certain . . . narrowness of outlook, but with luck it's a narrowness education and experience can do something to rectify . . .'

I'm thinking: now, do I just deck the cunt straight off?

– or do I go in for a little psychological torture – do I make the spoddy little bastard volunteer for a kicking?

He's with this gang of flat-chested bitches and I could just . . . pick one at random and gently start massaging her arse, slide my hand up her thigh and she'd be there with this look of panic that would never quite leave her face again –

She'd be staring at him, not daring to scream, do something! do something! – and even though he's shiteing it, even though he's pissing himself – he'll have to step up to me –

And then when he does, the question is . . .

. . . to glass, or not to glass?

To glass, I think.

There are those who say that to open by glassing is a cheap, vulgar move, and . . . to those people, I say – I *understand* how you feel. And I'm glad you feel that way. Because it means that if we ever . . . encounter one another, you're gonna end up on your knees, screaming and covered in blood, and I'm gonna be laughing in your fucking face . . . which will be in bits all over the floor.

But the spoddy little bastard gives up on ever getting served and turns to lead his crew of skinny-necked freak children – several of whom I know and hate from schooldays – up and out from the pub, apparently on their way to some bijou little gathering with cheese and wine and sun-dried tomatoes on ciabatta –

And inspiration strikes. If I'm going to kick off with a spoddy little four-eyed bastard, why do it in a public bar, where mine host will think badly of me for disrupting his evening's business, and mine host's door supervisors may well leap on me and prevent me from giving the spoddy little bastard the attention he deserves? Why not do it in the comfort of the spoddy little bastard's home – and have the extra thrill of smashing up his poncy gaff?

So I get Shirl behind the bar to spot me a bottle of voddy, and I join the gang.

'You don't mind if I tag along with you,' I say.

This look passes between them: suddenly we are all back in school. I am the nasty school bully, and they are my gutless, bedwetting victims. For all their BAs and MScs and years out snorting opium and shagging ethnic in India, when you cut to the fucking crap they are still the same friendless twats, shiteing it in the face of the nasty school bully.

This one bitch forces a smile. 'No, Gar, we don't mind at all.'

The gaff, the party, is a fucking wreck, obviously – even before I've got to work on the place.

I decide to open by necking every last drop they've got before kicking off with the headbutts, the kidney jabs and the throat stabbings – first insult, then the injuries. So I move into the kitchen to inspect their bring-a-bottle collection –

Beautiful moment of po-mo epiphany. He comes to a halt.

And there she is. Hovering over the drinks, looking really not at home, knocking back a can of Fosters – in one – and just . . . and just a strand of amber nectar missing her mouth, streaking down her perfect throat . . . and as that little lager drip hits the scoop neck of her white cotton-Lycra-mix bra top, it blossoms, like a little . . . like a teensy-weensy little light-brown mushroom cloud.

And it wasn't even like she was what you'd call conventionally fit. She was major-league fuckable, but more glamour model than catwalk model. German porn more than Scandinavian porn. She was fuckin perfect.

So there I am, in this party full of tossers, five seconds ago just about to kick off and smash the place up, and now all that bad shit in my belly has vanished and I'm just thinking, oh my shiteing Christ, how do I get to fuck this chick?

Normally I'd just be like, 'Wanna drink?', 'Wanna another drink?' and fuckin 'How about it, then?'

But that's how you do it when you've got fifteen chicks lined up against a bar and you don't particularly give a shit what you end up copping off with so long as you cop off with something. This chick, though – with this chick, I've got to get *her*.

It's not like I haven't gone for specific chicks before – like for a bet, or to piss some fucker off by bagging his bitch. What you do is, you just start talking and you ask her about work or if she's going on holiday or whatever, and when she starts rabbiting on first you just look her straight in the eye like you're really fucking riveted, and then after about five minutes you let your gaze slide away over her shoulder, and she gets panicky. She keeps talking but she's really checking out your threads, realising you're a pretty fuckin hip and happening guy and she's just some third-division smalltown minger, and she looks a bit of a twat to be even trying it on with a body so obviously out of her sexual league –

And then you swoop back in, you brush your hand against her arm, and you really quietly tell her someone walked by who was the absolute spit of somebody really close to you who died, and she'll be *so fuckin grateful* you weren't just bored shitless with her and so impressed with what a sensitive motherfucker you are, and she'll start on about some bastard she vaguely knew or perhaps just fucked who died of smack or AIDS or being stabbed in the neck, and as she gets into her story you look away, not over her shoulder this time but down at the floor with this dead-pained expression on your face. She won't notice for a second that you're not really listening, and when it does hit her, when she sees the look on your face she'll reach out and say, what's wrong, what's wrong, and you'll say, look, it's OK, right, it's just . . . it was my brother Dai what died, and he actually died of AIDS or smack or whatever she was talking about – and she'll feel like such complete shit that she'll go down on you right there and then; even if her bastard boyfriend is sitting in the fucking room, that bitch is eating out of your lap, no worries. And if you ever want to shag her again, you can: you just have to be a total cunt to her, and she'll be all – I know there's this sadness in him, if I could just get him to open up to me again, if only . . .

But as I'm watching this perfect chick wipe the Fosters from her chin, I'm thinking – that's not gonna work here.

'Cause there was something –

It was just this way she had of looking, see. She –

Christ, I'd say she looked like flowers, but flowers look like shit, really. She looked like –

Like on a really fucking sweltering day, your pits are drenched with just the effort of reaching up to open the front door, and you're dying for a drink but you're fucking broke, so when you pass the pub you try not to look in,

'cause you're only torturing yourself, but you can't help it.
So you look – and you see this crew of little shits sitting by
the window and maybe you just laid off kicking them in a
couple of weeks ago, and so you wander over and they all
start pissing themselves, and they rush to buy you a pint, just
to keep on your good side. And you're sitting there with
your pint on this sticky table, you reach out and take a good
swig, maybe two fingers so maybe an eighth of the pint is
gone already, but you've still got seven-eighths of the pint
left, and it's a classy pint, something triple-brewed and chill-
filtered, and the fizz of it in your throat beats any baking-
soda buzz, and it scours every little rotting crevice in your
mouth, making your mouth a place where some lager-
drinking glamour model might actually want to spend some
time, and as the fizz settles down in your stomach you've
still got seven-eighths of that pint sitting there, still almost a
full pint and just a couple of degrees above zero . . .

A moment like that – it can turn your whole day around.

Beat.

This chick looked like that moment.

So I couldn't just go up and talk all my usual shite, could I?
'Cause this was just . . . not the usual shite that comes along.

I was stuck. There was this moment, this thing dying to
happen, this fucking perfect chick standing right in front of
me and I was just standing there like a fuckwit, and
eventually, in due fucking course, she was just gonna turn
her back or maybe wander out the back for a fag, and I'd be
left there knowing it had all been that bastard close and –

And then, sal-fuckin-vation. The spoddy little bastard from
the pub comes stumbling up to the perfect girl, grabs a
bottle of lager, opens it – like a tosser, faffing around with an
actual bottle-opener rather than biting the cap off or
slamming it against a radiator – and then he – he tries to
fucking talk to her.

And I think – you fucking STAR. Who the fuck needs chat-up lines when you've got overwhelming physical superiority on your side?

I saunter up, casual like, and say to the perfect girl –

'Is this fuckwit bothering you, love?' And the spoddy little bastard actually jumps. He's just about to take a swig of beer and his hand freezes, caught halfway to his mouth. He turns round, the creepy little smile vanishing off his face, and looks at me, not quite believing what's gonna happen to him, babbling –

'I wasn't, I wasn't, I don't want any trouble, I was just *talking to her*, for God's sake.'

'And why the fuck,' I say, 'would a quality chick like this want to talk to a stupid little fuck like you?'

And he just . . . does *this thing*.

He gestures – tears on the bastard's cheeks.

The worst that's gonna happen is he's gonna get a mild kicking – and he's just there . . . like a fucking baby in front of this girl. I can't stand for that. So I'm gonna have to leave, which I really don't wanna do, or I'm gonna have to –

What I do is, I grab the bastard's bottle, and make like I'm gonna slam it in his face – but then stop like two inches in front of his nose, so the beer splashes all over him. He's standing, beer dripping down him, looking like a fucking twat, but at least you can't tell he was actually . . .

At least if his eyes are red he can say it was the beer.

And so there I am. Just me and the perfect girl. I'm looking at her, and she's just standing there, looking at me, and one of us is gonna have to say something but neither of us wants to say anything shit, in case it ruins the moment, but at the same time neither of us is walking away or getting embarrassed, we're just . . . waiting.

And finally, she says:

'Cheers for getting rid of that twat for me.'

And it's perfect, isn't it. It's like – not too complicated, not too simple, it's not saying too much, it's just – saying what needs to be said. And we both know what is *actually* being said.

So I'm like, 'Fucking no problem at all, love, any fucking time. I just can't stand to see men being disrespectful to a lady, like, won't fucking stand for it.'

'Well,' she says, 'you're a real gentleman, aren't you?'

'So,' I say, 'what's your name, love.'

'Mary,' she says.

To the rhythm of 'Mary, Mary Quite Contrary'.

. . . Mary. Mary, Mary . . . pretty as a fairy.

'I know what you're thinking,' she says.

'What,' I say.

'You're thinking – fucking *Virgin Mary*, aren't you?'

'No,' I say, 'no, I wasn't thinking that at all. I was just thinking what a lovely name that is.'

'Really?' she goes. ''Cause that's what everyone says – Virgin Mary. Or Virgin on the Ridiculous. Or Bloody Mary, my dad calls me – 'cause he always says, ten minutes of me and he needs a bloody drink.'

'Does he?' I say, laughing – laughing, and thinking, oh, does he? Remind me to give him a fucking slap next time I see him, he won't be such a fucking comedian then.

'So,' she goes, 'you gonna tell me your name, then, or am I gonna have to fucking guess it or what?'

And then my fucking phone goes and I'm grinning at her and apologising like a fucking twat as I'm trying to remember which pocket the bastard thing's in, and I get it out, and it's fucking Janey, and I'm like –

'Janey, for fuck's sake, what do you fucking want?' and she's all, 'Where you been? What you doing?' So I tell her, 'I been taking care of business. Obviously.'

'Oh,' she says. 'Can you come over? I been all on my own with the babby for ages.'

'No, no, I fucking cannot.'

'But I haven't seen you for days –'

'Actually, Janey,' I say, 'I'm in the fucking middle of something, if you must know, so I gotta go. All right?'

She doesn't say nothing, hoping I won't hang up on her when she's throwing a strop. But I do.

'Now, where was I?' I ask the perfect girl.

'You were just about to tell me your name,' she says.

'Oh yeah,' I say. 'Let me give you my card,' and I whip one out.

'"Crazy Gary's Mobile Disco",' she says, 'is that you, Crazy Gary?'

'Well, yeah,' I say. 'It's a professional name, obviously. I'm not really called Crazy Gary. It used to be "Craig and Gary's Mobile Disco", I used to do it with my brother Craig, but then . . . we fell out, and – he had to leave town. And the van had "Craig and Gary's Mobile Disco" on the side, and I thought, fuck, I'm going to have to get that all resprayed – but then I realised, I could just change the "Craig and" to "Crazy", and then it would say "Crazy Gary's Mobile Disco". And so, Crazy Gary was born.'

'Right,' she says.

'Yeah,' I says. 'I did the respray job myself. I looked at it and thought – fuck you, all the teachers in the world who said I was thick, 'cause that was a fuckin smart piece of respraying. Plus, fuck you, because you are teachers, who are twats who wank off thinking about schoolgirls in their little navy gym slips: whereas I've got my own fucking disco, and I get to wank off all over schoolgirls in their little navy gym slips, every fucking weekend if I want to.'

'Right,' she says. Just 'right'. Not actually sounding that impressed. Five seconds ago – that smile. And now – nothing.

Was it – that I got a van?
Was it that I got a disco?
Was it . . . that I got a *brother*?

Beat.

It was the stuff about wanking off over underage girls, wasn't it. 'Cause loads of chicks find that sort of stuff a little bit . . . they just don't really dig it *that much*.

So I tell her: 'Look, what I said just now, about wanking over chicks in school uniform. I don't really do that. I think it's sick, it's fucking disgusting. And I've never been with an underage girl. Except obviously a couple of times when I've been pissed, but they've always *looked* old enough to be legal.'

'Who hasn't made that mistake,' she says. 'And as it happens, I think dressing up is a laugh. I've kept all my school uniforms specifically for, you know – sex games, basically.'

'Really . . . '

'Oh yeah,' she says. 'I think it's dead sad when people can't explore and express the really filthy, depraved, extreme sides of their personalities within a consensual sexual relationship. It makes for crap shagging, for starters.'

'Well, yeah,' I say. 'I'm just the same.'

This chick really is it. I don't even have to bullshit her about all my little perversions – she's . . . *just like me*, for fuck's sake.

Beat.

It was fuckin Janey, wasn't it? I mean, I'd be fucked off if she was blabbering away on the phone to some other fucker while I was trying to crack on to her, for fuck's sake –

'That was Janey on the phone,' I tell her. 'She's like – my sister-in-law. She wanted to see if I could come over and – babysit.'

'Oh, yeah?' Mary says.

'Yeah,' I say. 'I mean, I fucking love her kid – I'm fucking great with kids, by the way – but Jane, she like – she never *thinks*, you know, phones me all hours telling me the kid's done this or the kid's done that, or wanting me to come over. Never thinks, like, that I might have other things to do. I'm not like, shagging her or anything.'

'Right,' is all she says. And still no smile.

And I say, 'It's just, you looked a bit, you know, not that impressed. I gave you my card and usually chicks are impressed I've got me own business, and you weren't, so I thought – fuck. What've I done? So I put two and two together, and thought maybe you were getting a bit jealous, like, of me talking to some other chick while I'm chatting you up.'

And she says, 'No, it wasn't that. It was just – I thought I recognised you, off the telly. I thought you were that rugby player, whassisname.'

'Yeah, a lot of people do say that. I do look like him. And I did used to play, when I was a kid.

'They thought I was gonna be the saviour of Wales. But I got this groin strain just before a match, Wales Under-18s v. England Under-18s, at the Arms Park. I couldn't let the boys down, obviously, so I went on, scored the try that won us the match ten seconds before the whistle. And my groin was permanently fucked. I had to give up the game that could've made me a bastard household name.'

'For real?' she says.

'Hey,' I says, 'do I look like the kind of bloke who'd lie just to impress a chick?'

'Well, fuck me,' she says. 'That's really fucking tragic.'

'Yeah, I know,' I say. 'You see the state of Wales now, they could've fucking done with me.'

'No,' she says, 'I mean you.' And she steps towards me, and just puts her hand lightly on my arm . . .

'If only I'd been there. I do, like, massage and stuff,' and she brings her face very, very near to mine, and whispers, 'I could've sorted your groin out for you.'

And when she says it, I mean, it's like a come-on – fair enough, obviously it's a fucking come-on – but it's not *just* a come-on, you know?

She like – actually fucking means it.

She says, 'So, no, I wasn't jealous of Jane. Because . . . Jane's not going home with you tonight, is she?'

She steps back, necks the rest of her can, and smiles at me. 'Right,' she says, 'I'm just off to the toilet to freshen up,' she says. 'Don't go anywhere.'

And I wanna come back with some dead snappy line like, 'I won't go anywhere, lovely, cause I can't, 'cause I can't fucking walk, 'cause I've got a hard-on the size of a fucking fire-extinguisher.'

But I don't.

I just blink.

I just blink, 'cause I've got some grit or something in my eye, and it's making them water.

'Fucking typical,' I say, 'a moment like this. And I get something in my eye, for fuck's sake.'

'Yeah,' she says, 'fucking typical,' and she goes off to the toilet.

So I'm standing there like blinking and wiping my eyes for I don't know how long, just people bumping into me – I say people, I mean fucking tossers, of course – and usually I'd like bump them back, but I just stand there.

And finally as she comes out of the toilet, she's walking back towards me and this ugly little bastard comes up to her, this shortarsed little shitehawk comes up to her, and he actually grabs her, and I think, I *should* put that fucker through the window and then go outside and stamp on his fucking face till there's nothing left of him – but I just feel sort of sorry for the poor bastard.

I just think – you tragic little twat. I pulled the perfect girl, and there you are, you can see her, you can smell her deodorant, you can even touch her arm –

But you're never gonna fuck her. What must it be like, to be such a fucking gimp, and see perfection, and know you're too much of a shitehawk to ever have it?

My phone goes again.

'Janey, what the fuck do you want?'

And she's all, 'Can't you come over?'

'For fuck's sake, Jane, I'm –'

He turns.

'– I'm doing a deal here, for fuck's sake, and it's not fucking helping having you make me look like some pussywhipped little shit, all right?'

And I don't wanna hear anything she's gonna say in response to that, so I put the phone down on her.

He turns back.

And she's gone. Mary's gone.

I run round the fucking party, and she's nowhere. I grab the spoddy little four-eyed bastard.

'Where's that girl,' I say, 'and don't say what girl, or I'll fucking put you through that fucking wall.'

And he goes, 'She left.'

'What?'

He starts whimpering.

'She left. With that guy she was just talking to.'

I punch him, obviously. 'No she fucking didn't.'

'OK then,' he goes, 'she didn't.'

I punch him again, and because he's wailing by now I cut my fucking hand on his nasty little teeth, and that really pisses me off, and he's just going 'I'm sorry, I'm sorry,' so I butt the bastard and let him drop to the floor.

On the street, there's no one. MARY! I'm actually screaming MARY! 'Cause I can see all this stuff, all this Hollywood shit, and it's all slipping away from me. MARY! MARY! I run down the fucking street, I can't see her. I run back the other way – there's no one there. I lose it, I run just down fucking alleys not knowing where I am, screaming MARY, MARY –

But my fucking legs are fucking killing me and it hurts like fuck to breathe, and I'm on my knees, I'm collapsed, I'm chucking up from the effort, and I've fucking fucked it up again, I've let her get away, I've fucked it up. I've fucked it up again.

And I'm on my knees, slumped against a wall.

And I put my hands to my face and when I take them away again they're wet.

And I think, but of fucking course. Of course this is how it works out. She just fucking vanishes off the face of the earth. What the fuck else do you expect?

What the fuck else do you expect, when you got all this bad stuff, all this bad stuff growing in your belly. That's not just gonna go away, is it? That's there for ever. Nothing's gonna get rid of that. And you are a fucking twat if you think any little bitch is going to get rid of that.

I rub my eyes.

In the shadows, over the road, I see –

I see that shortarsed fucking shitehawk who took her away from me. And it occurs to me, I should drag myself to my feet and get on over there and fuck him up.

But what's the fucking point of that? What the fuck will that even *do*? The bitch is gone, as if a fucking bitch could do anything.

And so I close my eyes –

And when I open them I'm on the other side of the road and I've picked him up and slammed him against the wall and I'm screaming at him, and I'm gonna take his fucking face off, I'm gonna castrate the fucking bastard – and I can see he's screaming but I can't hear it, I can't hear nothing –

And I blink, and when I open my eyes, I've let the fucker go, and he falls. He falls straight to the floor, doesn't even try and stay up. And I see how if I just bring my boot down on his face in the right way, it'll bring this all to an end, and so I wait for just a moment for his vision to clear, so he'll understand what I'm doing to him isn't an accident, it's a very deliberate response to that awful broken look on his face –

And my phone goes.

'Janey,' I say, watching his eyes crack open, 'I'll be round to sort things later but I've just gotta finish something right now –'

And she says, 'Sorry to disappoint, but it's not Janey.'

Beat.

'What the fuck d'you want,' I say to her.

'I knew it,' she says.

'What?' I say.

'Fucking typical,' she says. 'I knew you'd be like this.'

'Well, what the fuck d'you expect,' I says to her. 'One moment we're chatting and getting on nicely, the next – you've fucked off for no reason.'

'I fucked off for no reason. That's what happened, is it?' she says.

'Well, yeah,' I go.

''Cause let me tell you what happened from where I was standing,' she says. 'From where I was standing, we were talking.'

'Right.'

Gary *says nothing.*

'But the talking wasn't what it was about.'

Gary *says nothing. She goes on.*

''Cause underneath the talking, I was thinking – fuck me, something's happening here.'

Gary *says nothing. She goes on.*

'Something pretty fucking massive. But I wasn't sure, 'cause when can you ever be sure about other people.'

Gary *says nothing. She goes on.*

'But then you told me this really tragic story about your groin getting fucked up and I said I wished I could've been there to help you –'

'Yeah,' I says to her, 'and then you pissed off with some little shitehawk, didn't you.'

'You fucker,' she says. 'I wasn't sure, 'cause you never can be, and then you told me about your groin getting fucked up and then I said I wished I could have been there – and then what happened?' she says.

'I got some grit in my eye,' I tell her.

Beat.

'Well, ta-ra then, Gary.'

'Don't go –'

'It's been really fucking disappointing getting to know you –'

'OK,' I says to her.

'What?' she says.

'I didn't have no grit in my eye,' I says to her.

'Well, what then?' she says.

'They just filled up, didn't they.'

'With what?' she says to me.

'With water,' I says.

'With what?' she says.

'With tears,' I tell her.

Beat.

''Right then,' she says. 'In that case, I don't think we need to waste any more time, do we?'

'No,' I says.

'Get down the Boar's, and give's a call when you get there. I'll come and meet you.'

The kid is still crying to himself on the floor. I go over to check he's all right and he thinks I'm gonna have another go 'cause he curls himself up. And starts crying again.

And there's nothing in me – not a single tremor, not the hint of reflex spasm – that wants to grind his face into the floor.

And all the bad shit in my belly, that's just gone, it's like it belonged to someone else entirely, some poor sod who's gonna spend his whole life prowling around the streets kicking, and cutting, and stabbing – until the day the shit catches up with him, and finally he has to pay.

That poor sod isn't gonna be me. I'm getting off the streets right fucking now. There's just seconds to go. Seconds from now, and I'm going to be home, and safe, in the arms of the perfect girl.

2: a righteous brother

Mathew D. Melody *swaggers on stage, occasionally spraying his throat from a little water bottle to keep it nice and moist.*

A tense man – an executive, a vice-president – arrives home from work. As his sports car pulls into the drive, his wife looks up from her gin and weekly magazine, and sighs. She stands, walks upstairs and changes to go out. She dresses absent-mindedly, as if she no longer cares for how she looks, as if she were a lowly waitress at a dimestore diner throwing on a faded uniform – and yet she's putting on a thousand-dollar dress, and a string of the finest pearls.

They drive to their country club and are shown to their customary seats in the cocktail lounge. The drinks arrive – pink gin and the driest of martinis – and it's then that I take the stage.

I look at them, and I see: a woman so exquisite she can bear no ornament beyond her simple string of pearls, with an elegant, noble man in a crisply tailored suit. I see a modern tragedy unfolding before my eyes. I see a sweet young boy and –

– the perfect girl, and I see . . . that they have forgotten they are in love.

I greet the crowd, nod to the band-leader, and as the band strikes up, a love song – something simple and classic – I close my eyes . . .

. . . and I cut out a little of my heart, and give it up to that . . . exquisite lady.

Mathew *sings the Billy Joel classic, 'She's Always a Woman'.*

As I sing, she forgets the drink, the club, even the man she came in with: there's just she and I, walking on a distant tropical beach at sunset, as I sing for her. The balmy air fills her lungs, she hears the rustle of the sea breeze through the palms . . .

. . . and she feels love again, as fresh as when it was first love. She feels love again, as if it *were* first love.

The music ends; I bring her gently back to earth. She wakes from the song, light-headed, dizzy with shock, and . . . she looks into the eyes of her husband. She looks into his eyes, still drunk on the scent of that tropical night, and she falls in love with him all over again. And she forgets I even exist.

That piece of my heart which belongs for ever to that exquisite lady breaks as, before my eyes, they melt into one another.

I do that. I make that happen with a song. I strip away the greyness, the deadness, and I sing love back to life. I know your world is drained of colour and glamour, but try to imagine mine. Try to imagine that joy.

I finish my tale. The young woman sits back and regards me coldly. She says:

'Well, that's as may be, Mr Melody, but the fact remains – you've been unemployed for twenty-four months and you haven't found work as a professional cabaret singer. Now, there are some store assistant positions become available at Tesco's – can I get you an application?'

I say to her, 'No. You cannot.'

She says, 'Well, I think you really should consider it, because these positions require no previous experience nor qualifications. I can arrange an interview for this afternoon; you could be on the shopfloor this evening stacking away and tonight you can be out having a drink with the boys to celebrate your brand-new job.'

'That's no good,' I tell her. 'I shall be rehearsing all afternoon for a very important showbusiness engagement this evening, after which I will be taking my beloved Candy to dinner.'

She scowls at me. 'If you won't even apply for a job which you could in fact do, Mr Melody, then it's clear you're not really seeking employment at all. And then it's my duty to tell you that while I don't make the law, Mr Melody, I do enforce it, and so I'll have to be putting a stop to your benefits.'

I say: 'Look, Ms –'

And I want to call her by her name, because she's been handling mine rather roughly throughout this whole conversation, but I can't quite read it because the print on her badge is very small –

So small I have to – squint and screw my eyes up to make out what it says – Ms . . . Bunion? Bungle?

And she screams at me!

'Will you stop staring at my breast!' she screams.

Except she doesn't use the word 'breast'. She uses a word rather coarser than that.

For a second I am too stunned to speak.

Me – as if – I would never stare at a lady's – never! I mean – what would my mother say –

I reach out over the desk, just meaning to comfort her – and she jumps back, knocking her chair over.

'Don't you dare lay your filthy flippin' fingers on me,' she says, except she doesn't use the word 'flippin'.

'I'm sorry,' I tell her. 'I'm so sorry, but I really didn't do anything wrong, you know. I didn't.'

One of the lady's fellow workers comes over, a big man, and he grabs me, without listening to a word I have to say on the matter. He carries me out of the office and deposits me none too gently on the pavement.

It's at times like this I feel like giving in. Sitting in a puddle on the pavement, kids whizzing past me on all sorts of boards and blades, all of them laughing, none of them stopping to help . . . red and wet and cold, and all on what's supposed to be the most important day of my life so far.

How would I feel – if my beloved Candy saw me now, how would I ever live down the shame?

I pick myself up. Through the window of the Job Centre I can see the lady, with people crowding round her, comforting her. I tap on the window to try and apologise.

Mimes as he speaks.

I didn't mean to stare

Points to his eyes.

at your breast,

Cups his hands in front of his chest.

all right?

Then gives a thumbs-up.

But the nasty man starts to come outside again, and I scarper.

As I'm running, I remember what my mum says – to understand all is to forgive all. So what I do is, I go to a newsagent's and buy a nice card with flowers on the front, to try and explain.

Dear . . . Job Centre Lady,

I really didn't mean to stare at your . . . chest today. If I seemed like I was being a little bit odd, well, my doctor did say I might be, and I know I was late coming to sign on, because I overslept, but I hardly got a wink of sleep last night.

First, that lady from downstairs – who is ga-ga, as the direct result of stacking shelves for Mr Tesco – her cat was scratching at my door. I shouted at it to go, but it just wouldn't. It went on and on, scratching and mewling, and finally I'd had all I could take. I took the chain off, opened the door, and said to her: look, little cat, if you don't lay off scratching my door, I'm going to lose my temper with you – and then there'll be no telling what I'll do.

It stared me in the eye, as if it was thinking about answering back – but then thought better of it, and went prowling off down the corridor.

I got back into bed, and counted Frank Sinatra songs with the word 'love' in the title, and as I finally got to nodding off –

There's them next door. Rowing again.

And fair enough, it's not that loud. Fair enough, it's not like I couldn't put the radio on to cover it up but it's not just the sound, you see.

It's the knowing.

The knowing that just in the next building there's this couple. Tearing each other's hearts to pieces.

The noise I could ignore. But the *tragedy* . . .

I buzz at their front door. There are footfalls on the stairs, and the door opens.

'It's just,' I say, 'I've got an awful lot on tomorrow, I wouldn't dare to intrude normally.'

She's wearing just this little slip of a thing you can basically see straight through.

'It can't be doing you any good,' I say, 'shouting at each other like that.'

'I shout at him,' she says, 'because he peeves me off.' Except she doesn't say 'peeves'.

'Well, have you ever thought,' I say, 'that he might have an awful lot going on. In his mind. And if you tried to see things from his point of view, you might understand him better, and then you might not argue so much.'

She stares at me and chews at her lip.

'You know you're right,' she says. 'I'll do that; and you know, he'd be really touched by you thinking about us. Why don't you come on up and tell him what you've just told me.'

'Best not,' I tell her. 'But I've brought you this little pamphlet, it's got Bible stories in it about counting your blessings and how love is the greatest blessing of all – which many couples have found helpful –'

'Oh, go on, come up,' she says. 'See, the thing is, we argue because afterwards we get to make up.' And she leans forward to take my hand, and the strap of her little slip falls down her bare shoulders. 'Why don't you come and help us. You like that sort of thing, don't you.'

Back in my room I try and say a prayer for them: that the parables will do the trick and whatever is tormenting them and troubling them is fixed soon, and ideally within the next twenty-four hours, as I don't want to have to go through another night of banging and crashing next door – but try as I might I can't concentrate on praying because –

Because the scratching starts again!

I get up, open the door, and the cat is there, peering up at me.

I speak to it in the strongest tones I can muster. 'That's it,' I tell her. 'I've had about enough. You'd better leave me in peace – or I'm going to go downstairs and get your mother up and tell her how naughty you're being – and I don't think she'll be very happy being woken up at this time of night, do you?'

But this cat – looking me right in the eye – she raises her paw –

and then lashes out, and drags her claws right across my shin –

and I kick out.

I kick out, and send her flying.

She hits the wall, and – you know how they say cats always land on their feet? Well, she doesn't. She just hits the wall, and . . . sort of slides down it, and then . . . hits the floor.

I'm not normally like that at all, I'm normally the most placid person you could hope to meet, or so my mum says, but the doctor did tell me that I might be a bit short-tempered for a while.

'Well,' I say to the cat. 'That's what you get, isn't it.'

She doesn't move. 'I said, that's what you get for scratching, isn't it.'

I go over to her. She's breathing, but she isn't moving . . . and there's . . . there's this little string of blood out of the side of her mouth.

'You'd best go home now, little cat,' I tell her.

But the blummin thing just wouldn't move.

So, I got a cushion, and put her on it, and brought her into the flat. I put a little saucer of milk by the side of the cushion, but it didn't seem to spark her interest, so I put a tea towel over her as a blanket, and went back to bed.

But even then I couldn't sleep 'cause as she was breathing, the cat was making this wet noise, like she was gargling TCP, and it gave me the creeps.

And so, finally, at about five in the morning, just as dawn was starting to break, I managed to get off to sleep.

And then I overslept, of course, but – as I think you'll agree, Job Centre Lady – it was not really my fault, and so you cannot really blame me for being late to sign on today.

I had to buy a pretty big card to get all that on, I can tell you. And I close by saying:

And I'm sorry I was staring at your . . . chest today, only I wasn't, it's just I really wanted to know your name and you'd put your name badge on your chest, so where else was I supposed to look? Best Wishes, Mathew D. Melody.

I step outside the newsagent's – and a car drives past me at speed and splashes a puddle all over me and soaks me to the skin. A big, nasty car, which pulls up a few yards in front of me. I don't know the name of the model of the car because I've no interest in nasty cars driven by blummin *drugs dealers* – but I do know who it belongs to. Daniel Blister. Daniel blummin Blister.

Daniel Blister is not my best friend. Daniel Blister is a childish little pranny.

Daniel Blister . . . was going out with my beloved Candy when she met me and we fell in love.

I was sitting in a pub one night, having a quiet drink on my own at the end of the bar. There was this rowdy group, a stag party, on the other side, and this what I took to be a stripogram came in. But it turned out not to be a stripogram. It turned out to be Candy, doing singing telegrams. She struck up the old Righteous Brothers classic, 'You've Lost That Loving Feeling', and she had the most beautiful voice, I couldn't help but sit up and take note. But she had a cold or a dose of flu – her voice was straining and cracking, and in the end, it just gave out. And all these . . . yobbos were just laughing at her. And before I knew what I was doing, I'd picked up the song where she left off. I sang the song for her. And of course, they laughed. They laughed, but I kept on singing,

Sings the chorus to 'You've Lost That Loving Feeling'.

I finished the song, and they were still laughing – so I sang it again.

Sings the first line.

They kept laughing – I kept singing –

Sings the second line.

One by one, the yobbos fell silent. They ran out of laughter, long before I ran out of song. I had the whole pub under my spell.

After that, Candy asked me out for a drink to say thanks. And we just talked for hours. I told her about my singing, my gift, and I could tell she was impressed. We were both a bit nervous of each other that night, I think, 'cause we knew it was something special. She'd been seeing this guy – this Daniel Blister – but she knew she had to leave him the second she laid eyes on me.

And Candy and I've been seeing each other since then, once a week, every week, without fail. And that's –

Counts.

That's six weeks now. Every Thursday night. I don't see her a lot apart from that because she's got work and all, but we've *kissed* and everything, even though Candy's not the type of girl that really believes in kissing and stuff before marriage. She just says with me she can't help herself.

And I suppose it's just been really hard for Blister to come to terms with, because, you know, he's had to accept that Candy wasn't really in love with him like she's in love with me. Not at all. *Ever.*

But still: that doesn't excuse him being a childish pranny and a drugs dealer, does it.

So I walk home. Soaked to the skin when I start walking and soaked to the bone by the time I get there.

Now, outside my building there's a postbox. As I pop the explanatory note for the Job Centre Lady into it, I say a little prayer. I say,

Dear Lord God, Sorry about this morning an' all, but I have now made amends and I hope You will now accept my accounts are clear 'cause it is a big day for me and I know I haven't got a chance in heck unless You and all Your glory

is on my side. Lots of love, for ever and ever, Amen,
Mathew D. Melody.

And that's it. I'm set. My accounts are clear.

I open the door to my building –

– And I am hit by a flappy, wailing creature.

'Mathew, Matty-Matty-Matty, where've you been?'

It's the Ga-ga Tesco Lady from downstairs – and Nick
Weake, the warden.

'Mathew,' he says, 'I think we have a little problem-ette that
you might be able to solve.'

The Ga-ga Tesco Lady pipes up:

'Matty, Matty, my little catty has gone away! I can't find my
little catty!'

'Yes,' Weake says. 'You know cats, Mathew. They like to
get amongst the pigeons, and occasionally bite the pigeons'
head off.'

'Wendy's cat?' I say, and even though I know it's a sin to lie,
I say, 'No, as it happens . . . no. No, Mr Weake, I haven't
seen Wendy's cat for weeks.'

'Well, that's very interesting,' says Weake, 'because Wendy's
been doing a bit of detective work, and she says she detects
fresh cat hairs outside your door.'

The Ga-ga Tesco Lady nods at me emphatically.

'*Fresh* cat hairs,' I say. 'Well, perhaps we'd best take a look.
You never know, cats: they sneak around all sorts of places,
don't they.'

As I open the door to my flat I say a little prayer to the Lord
God to help me think of an excuse, but He doesn't help at
all. And of course He wouldn't, 'cause now I've told a lie, so
He's going to be in a moody with me again. The door

swings open and Weake pushes past me with the Ga-ga
Tesco Lady hot on his heels.

I wait for the inevitable.

Weake marches up, looking sternly at me.

'I'm sorry,' I begin. 'I can't really explain. The doctor said I
might be a bit odd but I know that's no excuse –' And
Weake cuts me off.

'It seems . . . I owe you an apology,' he says, like the words
cause him actual physical pain. 'It seems the cat is not in
your room.'

I go in and – the cat's vanished. The Ga-ga Tesco Lady's
starting to cry.

'Don't worry, Wendy,' I tell her. 'Your cat's probably just
gone exploring. Cats do that.'

'Exactly,' says Weake. 'Wendy, your cat has just gone a-
wander. OK? Cats go a-wander. They're hunters. They
walk alone. If you can't accept that and handle it in a stable
way, well, I'm going to have to recommend you're
forbidden to keep pets in future.'

Wendy nods and tries to force a smile – but it's the kind of
smile you smile though your heart is breaking; and they're
the most heart-breaking smiles of all.

'Wendy,' I say to her, 'Wendy, I'm very sorry about your
cat. Is there anything I can do for you to cheer you up till
you find her?'

And Wendy's face fills up with a smile. She points at my
stereo.

'Karaoke!' she screams.

'Karaoke,' I say.

She nods again.

Of course, if I give her my stereo, I won't be able to rehearse the biggest gig of my life and I'd be turning up cold, slack, unrehearsed . . . unprofessional. I mean what would Candy say?

Beat.

'Go on then, Wendy,' I tell her. 'You can have the stereo.'

And she grabs the stereo, and runs off.

Weake shouts after her, but she isn't listening. He turns to me. 'You stay there,' he tells me. 'I've got a bone to pick with you. I'll be back in precisely sixty seconds.'

I shut the door behind him and look around the room.

My suit is no longer laid out neatly on my bed, as I left it.

Somehow, it seems to have moved itself under the bed.

I get down on my knees and I see that my suit has somehow rolled itself up into a ball and then rolled under my bed.

I pull gently on the arm, and drag the ball out from under the bed.

I poke at it. It smells – bad.

I unfold the ball, and – the cat falls out on to the floor. It's not moving, and – it seems to have vomited –

There are all these –

– these red tubes coming out of the cat's mouth tied up with the ruffles on my shirt –

I suspect the cat may be dead.

I hear the door to the Ga-ga Lady's flat slam, and feet coming up the stairs.

I gather the cat up in my costume and run into the corridor.

'Mathew!' Weake shouts up the stairs. 'You stay right where you are.'

I duck into the cleaning cupboard and I have to . . . hold the cat and the suit very tight to my chest to get the door closed, and it . . . makes this gurgling noise, and stuff starts to seep out into my hands.

I hear Weake going into my flat.

'Mathew!' he shouts. 'Where the hell are you?'

I hear him walking into my bathroom, and I make a run for it.

I dash down the stairs – Weake hears me. 'Mathew, what the hell are you playing at?'

I run down the stairs, and into the entrance hall. I'm holding the Ga-ga Tesco Lady's cat wrapped in its own guts and my suit, and Nick Weake is coming down the stairs. He's going to see me and he's going to know, he's going to see it written on my face that I killed the blummin cat. I look around for some means of escape, but there's nothing, nothing, except . . .

Except the postbox outside our building.

The package of suit and cat is much too big to go through the slot, obviously, but . . .

But the cat *is* dead, after all. I mean, it's not going to know, is it? It's not going to suffer . . .

I run outside. There's no one around. I start to shove the balled-up suit into the slot –

And there are these cracking noises, as the little cat's bones give way –

– and blood or something spurts out on to the postbox but I hope no one will notice because the box is red anyway –

– and with a final shove and snapping and spurting the whole lot drops through.

Weake comes into the hall, and sees me, and marches out of the building.

'I told you to stay put, didn't I? Didn't I?'

'Yes, Mr Weake,' I say, 'but what with all the commotion I felt faint and I needed a breath of fresh air. What was the bone you wanted picking, anyway?'

He scowls at me.

'When I tried to gain entrance to your flat, Mathew, to look for Wendy's cat, I found my key didn't fit the lock. Now, I don't need to tell you, Mathew, do I? You do understand, don't you, that the whole point of this set-up is that I have keys and can gain entrance to tenants' flats at any time –'

'I know, Mr Weake. It's just – I don't like people being able to come in without telling me. My mum used to come in without telling me –'

He cuts me off. 'I can see that later we're going to have to have a little parental damage session about this. Book yourself in next week.'

'Yes, Mr Weake, thank you, Mr Weake,' I say.

I'm in a right state now, aren't I. I've given my stereo to the Ga-ga Tesco Lady and so I can't rehearse, and my suit's stuck in the postbox and even if I could get it out it's going to need a thorough dry-cleaning, and I've hardly got time for that. And the poor postman, he's going to open it up and there'll be this mess of black sequinned suit, dress shirt and thoroughly splattered cat. And then all the letters will be covered in blood and gore . . .

Including my explanatory note to the Job Centre Lady. If that gets all messed up then she won't understand and she won't forgive and my accounts won't be clear and –

This is NOT FAIR! I've tried my best to do everything and put everything right and it's all gone wrong.

Right.

That's it.

He gets down on his knees, clasps his hands, and closes his eyes.

Dear Lord God, I want words with You. I know I upset the Job Centre Lady but I did try to tell her everything in my explanatory note and still it's all gone wrong, and I know she hasn't actually had the explanatory card yet and read it and understood everything and forgiven everything – but it's not my fault if the post takes a whole day, is it?

He waits: then opens his eyes.

My mum told me, sometimes when you pray, all the little noises of the world put themselves together to make a little song . . . and that little song is the voice of the Dear Lord God.

He closes his eyes again, and listens intently for a while.

And there it is!

He sings in a priestly chant.

'Mathew, you didn't tell the Job Centre Lady the whole truth in your explanatory note, did you?'

What d'You mean, Lord. I did . . .

'You didn't tell her the real reason why you were late.'

Well . . .

I suppose I didn't, no . . .

'And that's why I let the note get all messed up, so you'd have another chance. And I hope you'll tell the whole truth and nothing but the truth this time.'

He leaps to his feet.

Right. Fine. I run across the street to the all-nite Spar and buy another card – even *bigger* this time – and I tell the Job Centre Lady the whole truth.

I wasn't just late because I overslept. The thing was, after I went to the doctor's, I was so proud I had to tell somebody, and who else to tell but for Candy, and so – I went round to Candy's place.

I pressed the bell but no one came for ages and ages. I was just about to give up when the door opened – and it was Candy. All glowing and bright and beautiful as ever.

'Candy,' I said, 'thank goodness you're in –'

And she cut me off. 'Mathew,' she said, 'what've we agreed?'

'I know, Candy, I know, but I've just been to the doctor's and he says I'm doing really well and so –'

And she cuts me off again. 'Well, that is good news,' she says. 'But you've spoilt it now, haven't you, coming here. I mean, here I am, spending the whole day –'

And a man walks by the door. In a dressing gown. And as he passes, he says to Candy, 'Cup of tea, love?'

Candy turns and goes, 'Yeah, it's in the cupboard above the sink. Two sugars in mine, please.'

Then she turns back to me.

'Here I am, spending the whole day making myself beautiful for you, and now you've spoilt it.'

'Sorry,' I say.

'Well, sorry's not good enough,' she says. 'I mean, I've got Jamie here . . . giving me shiatsu.'

'Oh, is that what he's doing,' I say.

'Yes,' she says. 'You may like me in them stilettos but they play havoc with my back. Every time I wear them for you, I have to get Jamie round to sort out my spine for me.'

'I'm really, really sorry,' I say.

'Just remember, Mathew: I'm a twenty-first-century woman. I need my space. If you can't accept that, then . . . '

And she slams the door in my face.

Well, after that, I couldn't really face anything. I went for a walk in the park. Then I bought myself a quarter of jelly babies and a bottle of Coke to cheer myself up. And even after I'd drunk it I was still in a moody . . .

. . . In such a moody I just dropped the empty bottle on the pavement, even though I knew full well that it was a crime.

And I carried on walking though I knew I'd done wrong, especially 'cause it was a glass bottle. I always get them 'cause I like the feel of them and the weight of them but you have to dispose of them carefully, because they can shatter and have someone's eye, it's the simplest thing. So I started back to try and find the bottle and put it in the bin but then I remembered I was late to come and see you, Job Centre Lady, and that's where it all started to go wrong.

By the time I've finished I've only got five minutes to get to the bus stop and catch the bus. But I'm set, I've done everything now, my accounts are all cleared.

Except . . . I might have made amends to the Ga-ga Lady for killing her cat, but what about the cat itself?

The bus is due any second – but I go over to the postbox –

Drops to his knees.

– to say a burial prayer for the cat.

> *'Ashes to ashes,*
> *Funk to funky,*
> *Hope you enjoy cat heaven,*
> *And sorry I killed you.*
> *Lots of love from Mathew D. Melody, Amen.'*

He gets up again.

And that's it, that's every last single thing.

I turn – and I see –

The bus.

My bus.

Speeding past the bus stop.

Without me on it.

No! That is *so* not fair!

And then a car pulls up. It's – Daniel Blister.

He sticks his head out of the window and says, 'Need a lift, mate?'

Well, yeah. I suppose I do.

Thumbs-up to heaven.

Dear Lord God – nice one!

So we drive to the pub. I walk up to the entrance and a bunch of kids are bustling their way out, and one of them's got a beer bottle and the bouncer won't let him take it outside, so I have to wait to get in and as I'm waiting I'm thinking – Daniel Blister making peace and giving me a lift to the gig. Daniel Blister saving my neck. Such are the miracles that come to your aid, with the Lord God and all His Glory on your side.

The kid with the beer bottle slips away from the bouncer, and throws the bottle up into the air. I'm thinking that of course the Lord God must be on my side now, 'cause I've taken care of everything. My accounts are totally clear.

The bottle sails through the air and spirals down towards the ground, where it will surely smash into a thousand pieces and do someone an injury before the night is through . . .

And there's nothing I've forgotten.

Not one single thing.

He falls to his knees, clasps his hands, eyes shut.

Dear Lord God, I'm really, really, really sorry about dropping the Coke bottle and littering Your beautiful creation, but if You can just fix it for me to win tonight then I promise I'll go straight round there and put it in the bin. Lots of love, Mathew D. Melody, Amen.

And I stay there, listening, just hoping to hear the song of God telling me it's going to be OK but –

– I don't hear anything.

I *feel*.

I feel this pressure on my shoulder –

– and when I open my eyes –

 – I see the bottle come spinning down and it swerves in mid-air, and it lands, perfectly safely, *in a bin*. And there's this man standing over me, tapping me on the shoulder, going, 'Pete, Pete,' he's going, 'Pete, I gotta talk to you, mate. I'm off, mate.'

I'm about to tell this gentleman I'm not the type who will put up with being called funny names – and I realise – that's it. People who *I don't even know*, coming up and wanting to talk to me – that's what happens when you're famous. It's a sign. It's a prophecy!

I push through the crowd, and there, stage-front, Candy is waiting for me, beautifully turned out in her best moleskin miniskirt and black leather basque.

'Where the – heck – have you been?' she squeals. 'He was gonna give your place to someone else!'

The compère is announcing me.

'Precious,' I say, 'you know I don't approve of such language.'

'I'm sorry, darlin,' she says. 'I was just worried about you. This is your day, and I was just worried about you.'

 'I know you were, darling, and it means a lot to me.'

'So . . . did you get to the doctor's?'

'Well, that's what I wanted to tell you,' I say. 'You're going to be very proud of me. The doctor said I was doing much better, and I told him you'd been weaning me off the pills, keeping them safe for emergencies. And so he said I could come off them if I wanted to: and I told him I wanted to.'

She stares at me.

'You what?'

'I told him I can get by without those crutches. I've got my girl and my music. And that's all I need. You've given me the strength to do without the pills.'

She's overcome with joy. 'You've done *what?*'

'I couldn't have done it without you, darling,' I tell her – and then the tape rolls, and it's my tune they're playing. I grab the mike from the compère's hand and jump on stage.

Croons at breakneck speed:

'YanevercloseyureyesanymorewhenIkissyuhlips . . . '

I settle into the rhythm.

Clicks his fingers lounge-lizard style, trying to find the beat, sings the next line.

And I look into Candy's loving eyes.

Except . . . they don't – look that loving. They're almost cold. Almost . . . contemptuous.

She's standing there, just in front of the stage, staring at me with these terrible cold eyes, slowly shaking her head . . .

I keep on singing but it has to be the worst performance of my life, cause I'm not feeling the music, I'm not even thinking about the music, I'm just thinking, Candy, Candy, what have I done wrong? How can you look at me with . . . *hatred* in your eyes? How? How?

My heart breaks.

I feel it breaking, like the ice on a lake when some little fat
kid tries to go skating. And as that cold stare burns into me,
I feel my heart freezing over, like the little fat kid turning
blue at the bottom of the lake, and I know I will never love
again.

The song comes to an end. Candy turns and walks out of
the pub.

I hang my head. My life . . . is over.

And the crowd erupts into applause. The compère puts his
arm around me, and there are tears in his eyes, and the
thick lenses of his red glasses magnify the tears so they're the
size of marbles, and in the marbles I can see little rays from
the spotlights, splitting up into all the colours of the
rainbow, like the rainbow the Dear Lord God sent to Noah
after the Flood, to tell him that the bad times were over and
everything would be good from now on.

'Mathew,' says the compère. 'You were tremendous in the
first heat, yeah, but that was spectacular. I don't think I've
heard such an emotional reading of that song – in my life.'

And I begin to understand.

'I don't think we need to,' he says. 'No. I don't think I can
bear to hear any more. Nothing I could hear tonight could
match that performance. That's it. That's it, everyone – the
competition is over. Mathew D. Melody – you are the first
ever Boar's Head Karaoke King!'

Mathew *sees the light.*

She pretended! Candy pretended! She *pretended* she didn't
love me any more – and scared me into giving the
performance of my life.

She put herself through that . . . *torture*. For me.

'Thank you,' I say to the compère. 'Thank you very much
indeed. But now, if you'll excuse me, I've got to go. First,

I've got to go and put a dangerous bottle safely away in a bin. And then I've got to go and find my true love.

'I've got to go and find my true love – and make her my wife.'

3: don't die just yet

Russell Markham: *in him, Jimmy Dean lives once again. He wishes . . .*

We were arguing. We must've been arguing, 'cause – what else do we do?

I said to her, 'Darlin, I've decided. I'm going. I'm leaving next week.'

And she thought for a moment, and said, 'Well, that's a pity. Billy at work was telling me about this holiday in Cyprus he saw on the teletext. Three hundred quid for a fortnight with as much as you can drink and your own en suite to throw up in.'

'Well,' I said, 'well, that is a pity.'

'Yes,' she said, 'it certainly is.'

I was a little surprised at how well she'd taken it, but I didn't want to push my luck. So I scarpered.

I jumped into the shower, and when I came out . . .

. . . She was there. On the phone in front of the telly. At the tail-end of a call, handing over my credit-card details.

'Darling,' I says to her, 'what's going on?'

'Well, it's a limited offer, isn't it. You act, or you miss out.'

'But,' I say to her, 'I thought I said –'

She gets up. 'Darlin, you didn't say nothing. You just implied it was impossible for you to move away next week, and come on holiday with me –'

She walks over towards me.

'– So naturally I interpreted that as meaning you were going to put off your departure, in order that we could go on holiday together.'

She cradles my face in her hands.

'Are you telling me, darling, that my natural interpretation of you was incorrect? Are you saying, darling, that I just . . . don't understand you?'

He crumbles, averts his eyes.

'No, I'm just saying – it's a pity, isn't it, that offers like that don't come up more often.'

'It certainly is a pity.'

She lets go of my face.

'You're looking a bit shaky, darling,' she says. 'Are you all right?'

'Fine,' I say. 'Just a bit . . . just a bit of a glucose crash coming on, I think.'

'Well,' she says, 'you go and get dressed, and I'll serve up. Bit of dinner'll sort your sugar levels out for you.'

She starts laying the table for dinner. I say, 'Darling, it's just, if I say I'm going to leave, then I kind of have to, don't I? I've sort of made a promise to myself, haven't I? It's like – a debt of honour.'

She doesn't even look up. 'Well, I don't see that at all, darling,' she says. 'There's no reason –' and she slams down my plate

'– why you should –' and she slams down her plate

'– go next week –' and she slams down my fork

'– rather than –' and she slams down her fork

'– in two weeks' –' and she slams down the salt cellar

'– TIME –' And she slams down the red sauce, the brown sauce, the butter dish and the toothpicks.

Russell *steels himself.*

'Well, darling –'

And then she does it. She looks up at me.

He crumbles again.

'Well, darling,' I say, 'I suppose you're right, aren't you. I mean, I suppose the whole idea of making a promise to yourself, it's just ridiculous. You know, a promise, it's like inherently something you make to someone else –'

She cuts him off.

'I just want us to have some proper time together before you go away. Sun, sand, sea and . . . other things that begin with "s". And you can bring your guitar and get a bit of practice in. Serenade me on the beach as the sun goes down . . . It'll be dead romantic.'

She hovers over me, thinking. She hovers, not dressed to go out yet, still in vest and combats and bare feet, thinking she's having private, clever thoughts, but even without looking at her face, just from the angle of her hand against her hip I can tell what she's thinking. She's thinking about jumping me. She's still thinking about jumping me as she heads back into the kitchen, favouring me with a sly backward glance just as the strap falls down her shoulder, as she brushes a stray lock of fringe from out her eyes, I can see it –

– even as she brings out the spuds I can see right into her brain, to the very bioelectric flows which *are* her thinking that, armpit stubble notwithstanding, she's looking pretty damn sexy in an unaffected, tousled sort of a way and maybe right now's the moment to take me by surprise and because maybe if it's by surprise then there won't be a chance for me to work up any performance-related anxiety and so maybe this time it'll all happen –

– and I want to shout at her, 'No! No! It won't happen, 'cause it won't be by surprise, because how can it be by surprise when I can already see you thinking about it, you dull bitch.'

But obviously I can't shout anything like that, so to head her off what I do is, I grab the paper, and as I do so I knock a neat stack of junkmail from the sideboard – and on to the floor. And of course I bend down straight away to retrieve the assorted handbills and flyers –

– but I leave one there.

A cheaply printed pamphlet, a religious tract. I leave that one right there on the floor.

She sees what I've done. Just left it there. On her clean floor.

And that tells her.

I sit back and dive into the paper, hoping for refuge from the dark looks that will be waiting for me if I dare venture a glance her way.

I milk some amusement from the desperate and lonely ads: 'Not Too Dull for Love', 'Mr Average Looking for Love' –

But then my eye, expressly without permission, flicks on to a story.

I read the story, and the ground shifts under me.

There's this bloke, lives on the council estate the other side of town. He is what they call a pigeon fancier. He's long been renowned within pigeon-fancying circles for the extraordinary homing skills of his pigeons: and now – in death – they're lending him a small measure of general-purpose local celebrity.

See, the bloke let his pigeons out for a little bit of a flutter, and only one of them came home. It came home in the post. In two separate Jiffy bags. Head in one, body in the other.

The bloke assumed some evil-doer who's savvy to the pigeon-fancying world had kidnapped his birds, and that a ransom note with threats and demands would follow; and that if he paid up – and never fear, he would've paid up – he'd get his pigeons back

Sure enough, the next day, the note came.

Except it wasn't a ransom note. It was more an . . .
explanatory note.

And, sure enough, he got his pigeons back. In a number of
blood-soaked Jiffy bags. All their necks neatly snapped.

So I turn to this rag hoping for a few cheap laughs at the
expense of the local Romeos. And I get this – blast from the
past.

I look up from the paper, and into her eyes. She's leaning
over the now comprehensively laid dinner table, regarding
me affectionately.

'Tuck in,' she says. 'You don't want to let it go cold, do
you?'

'I'm not eating it,' I tell her.

'And why not?' she says.

And I want to say: because I can't stay a second longer in a
town where this kind of stuff goes on.

I want to say to her: it's not about going off and making it as
a lovelorn sad-eyed star sailor with a guitar in my hand and
a million songs in my broken heart because, as we all know,
I'm never going to be any good at playing the guitar. My
fingers are too short and stubby, and I can't get them all on
one fret at the same time

I want to say to her: it's not about me going away to do
something. It's just about me needing to get out of this
fucking place.

'Why?' she says. 'Why don't you want to eat the dinner I
have lovingly prepared for you?'

'Because,' I tell her, 'because –

'– Because you've gone and done the mash all creamy
again, haven't you? You know I hate it when you do the
mash all creamy!'

'Well,' she says, 'you don't have to eat it then, do you, darlin. So long as you eat the rest of your veg.'

I sit there, and play with my unpleasantly creamy mashed potatoes, till I catch her staring at me. I take the hint. I lift a fork laden with mash to my mouth, I ram it home, and I swallow it all down.

'That wasn't so bad, was it?' she says, and smiles.

'No,' I say, and I smile back, 'and by the way, after dinner I've got to leave town.'

Beat.

'Well, I know that,' she says.

No explosion. No shouts of anguish. No incoming cutlery missiles.

I look up at her.

'Well, *of course* I know that,' she says. 'And do you know how come I know? It's because you've told me you've got to leave town about three or four –'

And for a moment it's like her mind disconnects and all the life goes out of her face, and I'm staring at her thinking, I understand now. You're an alien. You've been sent here to test the human male under stress conditions and are tormenting me not out of sadism but in the name of alien science – and when your mind drifts off like that in the middle of an argument, it's because you've gone drifting through a wormhole in the curled-up ninth dimension of spacetime to reach out to the motherworld and dump a particularly juicy new set of experimental data –

And then she slips back into normal space and picks up right where she left off.

'– I know that because, well, I won't say you've said it three or four hundred times a day, because that would be exaggerating, but three or four dozen times a day, definitely.

You've said it to me three or four dozen times a day, every day we've been going together.'

'So what do you *think* about me leaving?' I ask her.

'I think,' she says, and she just pats her mouth with her napkin –

Back to her voice.

'No, it's not a napkin, darlin, it's a serviette, because a napkin is a piece of cloth but this is paper, so this is a serviette, darlin –'

Back to his own voice.

– She just dabs at her lips with her serviette, and – why? Why would you do that? It's not like if there was any food stuck to your lips this genteel little dabbing would do a damn thing about it, you need a proper wipe, don't you, to get stuff off your lips, you need a good wipe to get your mouth clean.

So she dabs at her lips, and gets up, and says:

'What do I think? I think I would like some peaches and cream for my sweet, that's what I think. Would you like some also, darlin?'

'No, no, I do not want peaches and cream. I don't like peaches and fucking cream.'

'Well, your mum always gives it you every time we're round hers.'

'Well, my mum is a doddering old cow who never listens, isn't she. I don't like peaches, for one thing, and I don't like cream, for another.'

She stands, looking down on me.

'What's so wrong with this place, huh?' she says. 'I mean, you've got a good job.'

And I want to say to her –

Good job? Is that what you think? You think it's a good job, being a supermarket trainee manager, trainee under a glue-sniffing sixteen-year-old who gets write-ups in the local rag for his programme to employ mentally defective young ladies and thus reintegrate them usefully into the community . . . What the write-up does not mention is the real bonus of employing these confused young ladies is how handy they are for a crafty grope off in the warehouse.

But I don't say any of that. I just say, 'I'm leaving.'

'And it's not as if we're starving or freezing to death,' she says.

And I want to say – It's not that I'm starving, it's that I eat nuked 99p lasagne six nights a week and whatever's on special for Sunday. And I know I'm not freezing, it's just I can't concentrate on anything but the tick-tick-tick of the meter wheel speeding up whenever I do put the fire on.

But I don't say any of that. I just say, 'I'm leaving *tonight*.'

'And we've got our health, haven't we,' she says.

And I want to say – I know I'm not dying of some banal dehydration disease that could be bought off with a 10p mix of sugars and salt – but I also know that every day I live this shitty life is part-payment on some ultra-complicated physical or mental fuckup thirty years down the road. And when my name finally reaches the top of the fuckup waiting list, I'll actually be grateful. I'll reach down and fondle the tumour-roots growing out of my belly, and say: thanks, guys. Thanks for getting me out of this one.

But I don't say any of that. I just say, 'I'm leaving, tonight, right now.'

And she says, 'And we've got *us*, haven't we? And we love each other, don't we?'

And I want to say – If you knew. If you had half an idea what that word meant. If you even *liked* me or at least didn't hate me and just vaguely wished me well then you'd *help me* for fuck's sake –

He cuts himself off.

But I don't say any of that. I don't get a chance to.
Because –

She smiles at me.

She gives me this look that might become a smile. But then it hardens.

Into something . . . easier to manage.

'I can't believe you're going to let Mickey down. He's been planning this party for ages. And just cause of some stupid story in the paper.'

I get up.

'*Corrie*'s on, darlin,' she says. 'We always cuddle up and watch *Corrie* together.'

I don't say a thing.

'And I've just put the tumble dryer on,' she says. 'It'll be done in an hour – don't you wanna take your clean clothes with you?'

I go into the bedroom and realise if I'm going to pack I need a suitcase.

'You're just stressed out,' she says. 'I'll give you a nice back rub, calm you down.'

I find my suitcase under the stairs. I pull it out and drag it into the lounge. She follows me. She goes to follow me into the bedroom, but – she can't manage it. As she passes the sideboard she has to stop, even at a time like this she has to stop, and lean down and reach for that grubby little flyer I left on the floor to piss her off, and she has to pick it up and neatly fold it into halves and quarters and eighths before putting it away into a drawer.

'Listen,' she says. 'If you're gonna go 'cause of some stupid story in the paper, then before you go, I wanna tell you a story, and you've gotta listen. And if you listen, I'll let you go.'

'OK,' I say.

'OK,' she says. 'This story used to go around school when I was a kid, one of those stories you hear again and again, only with different names every time. The version I heard when I was in the second year was that Bungle caught a couple of first years going through his jazz-mag stash behind the metalwork block.

'Bungle offered the kids a deal. They could have the shit kicked out them really really badly . . . or they could provide a little entertainment for Bungle and his mates.

'Noting their interest in German porn, Bungle got them to pick out which picture they liked best, and said they had to jerk off over it with Bungle and all his mates watching and placing bets, or get every bone in their bodies broken.

'Now the first kid was a bit of a mummy's boy, and all he could think was that if he did what Bungle told him, he'd be so disgusting not even his mum would be able to love him any more. And if even his mum couldn't bear to love him, then he'd be alone, forever. And that would be a million times worse than being kicked in.

'And so the mummy's boy relaxed, because he knew what he had to do: 'cause he understood that when it was all over his bruises would fade and his bones would mend, and he would still be loved.

'But then the mummy's boy looked over at his friend. And his friend was shaking and crying.

'The friend was shaking and crying, because – for him, there was nothing worse than being kicked in.

Beat.

'The friend came in five seconds flat. Obviously appreciated an audience, Bungle said. But the mummy's boy was having problems. So Bungle made his friend . . . help him out. Orally, as it were.

And when the mummy's boy finally comes, Bungle says it's not fair one of the kids gets a mouthful and not the other. So he says the mummy's boy has got to lick his friend's jism up off the picture in the porn mag – that, or they'll both get their faces stamped on.

'And the mummy's boy does it. Not 'cause he's scared of getting kicked in by Bungle, but 'cause his friend is.

'The two kids promise they'll never ever tell anyone about what happened and never ever talk about it again.

'And they don't. They don't get the chance to. Because the mummy's boy runs away that afternoon and no-one knows what happened to him.

'The friend sticks it. He sticks it out and he never says a word. When the other kids laugh at him, he pretends he can't hear them. When the whole class teases him, he ducks his head in his book so they won't see he's crying. He sticks it out till the school finds something else to gossip about – which takes quite a while, as you can imagine.

'And,' she says, 'it strikes me, if a person didn't have the nerve to leave town after that kind of humiliation, well: that kind of person's never going to leave, are they? They might talk about it, and dream about it, and make plans about it . . . but they'll never actually find the nerve to just get up and go.'

Beat.

Am I right?

He stands, itches, licks at his lips, wipes his mouth.

'So,' she says to me, 'shall we go down the pub for a drink before we head on to Mickey's party?'

Beat.

In the pub we are instantly crushed. She vanishes and is back in less time than it takes to even walk to the bar with a round of drinks. She puts the first pint in my hand and leans close, and whispers, 'I put a double in it to keep you happy.'

I take a massive gulp and it doesn't do enough so I'm begging her: please stay with me, stay with me just this once – but she's off. 'Just a couple of friends I wanna talk to, darlin.' And she winks at me, and strides off, the crowd parting before her.

I'm like a twat, stapling my elbows to my sides, trying not to take up space, trying to present a low profile and avoid eyes but Mickey swoops in, wondering when he's gonna be able to sort me and the old lady out with a gorgeous little starter home on the new development and there's sweaty, hairless chicken flesh pressing against me from all sides and I've got to get away so I raise up my glass: and I down the pint, in one. If I can't leave physically, I can at least take leave of my senses.

As the glass reaches the horizontal the booze divides according to proof. The lager sinks down, floods my belly and reaches to my throat, while the vodka lurking at the bottom of the glass – which no way is a double, it's a triple, at least – the vodka floats up through the roof of my mouth, and washes through my brain,
bathing those battered synapses,
soothing my aching cerebellum:
making my head *all better*.

And this guy says, 'You were always brainy, I need to ask you something.'

And then she comes over. It's like she's been watching even though I haven't seen her looking my way once. She's spotted I've got someone to talk to and I'm not completely miserable and she's buggered if she's having that.

'We're ready to go,' she announces.

'Well, I'm just talking to my mate,' I tell her, 'and we just wanna have a little chat.'

'Well, I'm ready to go,' she says. She states.

I just look at her.

'I can't leave now, darling,' I tell her. 'My friend here wants to ask me something, and so it would be the height of rudeness to leave just now, wouldn't it?'

'Fine,' she says, 'I'll see you at Mickey's.'

And she flounces off.

'So,' I say to the guy, trying to keep a lid on it. 'So . . . what was it you wanted to ask me?'

The guy says, 'I want to tell you a story, and when I've finished, I'm going to ask you a question: is the story beautiful, or is it sad?

'The story runs as follows: I'm back in town for a friend's funeral. This friend of mine went to university and worked diligently and got a job straight after, pausing only for a brief summer break in France before getting down to his working life. He got this job that took him away from our town and all the obvious cities, out to a country in the Pacific Rim where he worked for a company that had a licence to print money. Everyone was surprised. We all thought this guy would go places – but spiritual places, saintly places. We all thought he'd do things for humanity, not for cash. But he just got rich, and when he was rich enough, he stopped. He took early retirement.

'And within a year of taking early retirement he was diagnosed as having terminal cancer.

'I went to the hospital to see him, and I said to the doctor, how come, doc? He was always so ferociously healthy. And the doc said, "Kid, it's a psychic thing. He's been carrying this cancer for thirty years, but he always had this passion for his work, and that kept fighting the cancer off. And then he lost what made his life worth living, and his body just gave up."

'So, nervously, I admit, because physical decay really does disgust me, I went in to see my friend, and I said, what the hell's up with you? If your job was keeping you alive, why the hell don't you just get another job?

'And then my friend told me the real and truthful story of his life.

'That summer in France between university and the Pacific Rim he met a girl, a perfect girl with blue eyes and copper hair, and they had an affair. It lasted just long enough for them to fall in love, but not long enough to argue or have a disappointing sexual experience. But this girl was engaged to some cheery, self-starting graduate hardbody and my friend was already booked on a flight to the Pacific Rim. My friend was willing to cancel the flight, but apparently this chick was not willing to cancel the engagement.

'And this totally fucked the guy up. Twenty-one, the springtime of his life, and he decides he's through with love. He devotes himself to the empty and soon-to-be-obsolete cash trade purely out of this huge existential sulk with the world.

'And what I need to know is: this obsession, your whole existence revolving around somebody you can never actually touch – is that beautiful, or is it tragic?'

*Back to **Russell***'s voice.

I don't even attempt an answer. I just make my apologies and back slowly away – but he grabs me and says, 'Look, you've gotta fucking answer me, OK, because of course, there is no friend, there is no guy, everything I've been telling you about, it's me, it's my life – I've wasted the last thirty years and now I've got cancer for a skeleton and only the fact that my blood has been replaced with liquid morphine is keeping me from going mad with the pain. And what I need to know is, this girl, this perfect girl who, if you

must know, had copper hair like a newly minted penny and
eyes as blue as a fiver – if I call her up and tell her my whole
empty life has been a tribute to her, no, not even a tribute,
it's just been a shell, a mould, a casing around the vacuum
where our love should have grown –

'– will she laugh at me, or will she think it's beautiful?'

I pull the guy's hands off me, and I say, 'What the fuck?
What do you mean, you've wasted the last thirty years?
You're the same age as me. We were at school together.'

'Yeah,' he says. 'We were at school together.'

'But you're fucking fifty,' I say to him. 'You're fifty years old
and you're dying of cancer.'

'Yeah,' he says.

'And that can't be,' I tell him, ''cause you're the same age as
I am. And I'm twenty-three.'

Beat.

I don't know how much later, my senses and I embark on a
tentative reconciliation.

I open my eyes, and I'm back at the flat. I'm on the floor, I
can't feel my legs my arms nothing, just this pain in my guts
like . . .

Beat.

OK. OK: the pain in my guts, is like this story that went
round our school, about these two kids, these two best mates
who got caught looking at Bungle's jazz-mag stash behind
the metalwork block. Bungle really just . . . did bad things to
them. One of the kids – a bit of a mummy's boy – had
wanted to fight Bungle: the other . . . didn't have the nerve.
The mummy's boy couldn't stand the shame, and – so the
story goes – ran away and no one knows what happened to
him.

The story's wrong, of course. His mummy knows what happened to him. The doctor that prescribed the sedatives knows what happened to him. The nurses that shaved his head . . . they know.

The other kid, the kid who didn't have the nerve to fight, he just sticks it out – so the story has it. Sticks out the teasing and the laughing and the name-calling.

But maybe the story's wrong about this kid, as well.

Maybe this kid who didn't have the nerve to run, didn't have the nerve to fight, maybe he had the nerve to wait.

Maybe after years of waiting the kid woke up one day and found out Bungle had been picked for the Under-18s team, picked to play against England. And maybe he called on a schoolboy classic; maybe he dosed Bungle's sandwiches with an immense amount of over-the-counter laxative.

And if that did happen, then when Bungle ran out on to the hallowed turf to represent his school and his nation, and the entire contents of his intestines moved abruptly and explosively into his shorts – that wasn't just a random tragedy, it was a carefully planned act of revenge.

So when Bungle ran from the field, back down the tunnel, a foul-smelling yellow liquid spilling from his shorts as he ran; and when the school, and the nation, lost, and Bungle lost his nerve, and never played again, and a promising sporting career was ruined – surely, that would be enough to settle the score. Surely all accounts would finally be cleared.

I come to – after what might be years – and I'm back in my flat; and in front of me is my suitcase. It is packed. I, apparently, have packed it. It seems I'm ready to go.

Except, of course, I can't go without saying goodbye, can I?

Because you can't just leave things like that unsaid, can you? You can't start something new when there's old business still to be sorted.

I walk into the party and Mickey says, 'Uh, hi. I, uh, your old lady's been working the crowd.'

And I say to him, 'Mickey, who the fuck talks like that? What's wrong with you?'

And he says, 'Look, it's just . . . I think – I think she's, you know, caught some action in your absence.'

And I follow his eyes, and I see her –

– talking to –

– this fucking –

– this beery cunt with a chunky gold choker –

– actually talking to this cunt with mangled teeth, and a drooling mouth, and a heavy, unbroken eyebrow crowning his perpetually broken nose, casting deep, deep shadows over the layered bags around his eyes –

– royal-blue bags folding into purple bags, which fold into dark-brown bags, which melt into his glassy, bottomless, granite eyes –

– and her assuming the classic pose – leaning slightly into the curve of his body, secondary sexual organs –

– presented, hand resting lightly on his forearm, whispering to him, lowering her voice so he has every excuse to lean in closer, so with every word her sweet breath caresses his left-over cauliflower ear –

– and, oh, the smile blossoming over his idiot face as she speaks –

And then she's at my side, saying, 'Honey, are you all right? Honey, what's wrong?'

And I'm just babbling, just – 'I can't believe what you're doing. I can't believe you'd – with that fucker!'

'Well, darlin,' she says, 'if you're gonna leave me, if you're gonna leave town, I'm gonna have to find someone to look after me, aren't I?'

I look up at him and his gaze swings around the room, and – I turn away.

'All right! All right,' I tell her, 'I'll stay. Just promise me you're not gonna go anywhere near that bastard.'

'I promise,' she says. 'I promise, if you're gonna stay.'

'I will, just – get me out of here.'

She helps me out on to the street.

'I know you must be shocked, darlin,' she starts, 'but I had to do something . . . to make you realise how much – just how hard it'd be for me if you left. I couldn't go on on my own. I'd have to have someone to look after me.'

We get to the flat. I always open the door, so she waits for me to pull out my keys. I tell her I haven't got them, I left them on the table 'cause I'm leaving now –

– And in her face there's a look of panic which I'm only just noticing and it strikes me that what she said about needing someone to look after her wasn't just a line to get me to stay. I mean, obviously, it was a line, it was a cheap cruel line, but – not just a line. She really is afraid of being on her own. Of me leaving.

'Honey,' I say to her, 'I'm not coming in with you.'

'But you promised,' she starts, 'you promised, you little shit, you lying little piece of shit –'

'I'm not coming in because you're going up to your flat, you're going to pack a bag, and you're coming with me.'

Her face freezes.

'You're coming with me. We're leaving this shithole tonight, and tomorrow –'

'You're not leaving me?'

And I smile at her. A real smile, for the first time in ages.

'I can't live here. You can't live without me. So we leave –
together.'

And she smiles back.

She runs up the stairs, in such a rush she forgets to close the
door behind her. The light goes on in her flat. I see her
silhouette moving against the window as she rushes around
the flat, getting her things together. And I'm thinking –
maybe this is it. All this time I've been trying to get up the
nerve to leave town on my own and perhaps all I needed all
along was – my girl.

And then the action upstairs stops.

She comes to the window. She leans out.

'Darlin,' she says. 'I can't decide what to take. Will you
come up and help me?'

'It doesn't matter,' I say, 'just pack a bag for a couple of
days. You can come back and clear your flat out when we're
set up, all right?'

She stares down at me.

'Darlin, can't we just stay tonight and go tomorrow?'

'No. If I stay another night in this shithole, I'll never get out.
I'm going tonight.'

Her face vanishes from the window.

She comes back. She says, 'Darlin, I'm just filling the bath.
I'm gonna get in. And . . . I'm gonna cut myself, and let
myself bleed. I'm gonna bleed to death, darlin, unless you
come up and save me.'

'I can't, honey,' I tell her. 'I can't come up. I haven't got my
key.'

'You don't need it,' she says, 'I made sure the door didn't close behind me. So either you come up, or I'm gonna bleed to death.'

And that's –

– when the bastard hits me. The first thing I know is I'm slammed up against the wall, my nose in bits sliding down my face and my mouth full of snot and blood, and then this cunt is punching hell out my kidneys, screaming, 'What the fuck've you done with her, you fucker? Where the fuck is she?'

I slide down the wall and crash on to the pavement.

'MARY!' he screams, 'MARY!

'Where the fuck is she? What the fuck have you done with her?'

And he's howling, he's howling like a little baby, 'MARY! MARY!'

And with blood in my eyes I look up and she's there in the window.

He steps towards me, screaming and spitting and –

– a phone goes. His phone goes.

He picks up, and talks. Then he leans down, brings his face very close to mine and whatever he's going to say I don't want to hear it I'd just rather die now please just let me die now rather than have to go through this and he opens his mouth and he says –

'Look, mate,' he says, and I look up and I see things have shifted under the surface of his face –

'Look, mate,' he says –

And I realise I can get out of this alive –

'Look, I'm sorry about that –'

– he wants something from me, and I can give it to him, and I can get out of this alive –

'– things just got a bit fucked-up –'

He wants me to look up at him, or shrug, or nod – and let him off the hook –

'Didn't mean anything by it, like –'

And he needs it, he needs this from me –

'And you're all right, aren't you? No hard feelings, like.' He finds the ghost of a smile as he offers me his hand. I just have to take his hand, and I can have my life back.

Except: I can't.

I can't. Because –

– Because of years of watching my best mate staggering round the place, a chemically coshed wreck of a man who doesn't even remember his own name, let alone mine: because of having to watch the poor bastard singing to himself in pubs and kneeling on streetcorners praying out loud and reading in the paper about him getting done for ripping the necks off fucking pigeons.

His hand hangs in the air, his eyes are pleading: and just by spitting in his face now or even turning away, I can get my fucking head kicked in – but I'll have paid the fucking bastard back.

Beat.

'Cheers, butt,' he says, as his knuckles crush mine. 'Fucking appreciate it.'

'You're all right, mate,' I hear myself saying, 'no fucking worries.'

He walks off, back towards town.

Beat.

I slump down on to the kerb.

At my feet, in the gutter, there's a Coke bottle. An old-fashioned one, a glass one. It glitters orange in the street lights.

The door to our building swings open. I feel the warmth from the central heating wasting, spilling out on to the street.

Beat.

I find him outside the Boar's, leaning against this crappy Escort van, swearing as he plays some stupid little game on his mobile.

He sees me coming, and puts his phone away.

'For fuck's sake, mate,' he says. 'I thought we were straight, like.'

I keep walking.

'I've apologised about smacking you, and if it's about the girl, then – tough. She wants me and there's fuck all you can do about it.'

'It's not about the girl,' I tell him.

'What?' he says.

'What did you just say?'

I take my hand from behind my back, and let him see the bottle.

He looks at me, and he's –

– disappointed. Disappointed in me.

'For fuck's sake,' he says. 'You don't wanna be doing that now, do you.'

I step towards him.

'Look, mate,' he tells me, 'whatever it is, whatever you think it is, you've got the wrong bloke, all right? It wasn't me.'

I smash the bottle on a lamp-post, and raise the jagged shards towards him. His face darkens.

'You didn't wanna do that. You didn't wanna fucking threaten me, you shitehawk.'

I say to him –

I don't say anything, my mouth's so dry I can't say anything, so I just take a step closer.

And he says, 'You didn't wanna fuckin do that, you shitehawk, unless you had the fuckin nerve to go through with it. And you fuckin don't.'

He steps towards me, all apologies gone.

'You don't have the fuckin nerve, boy. You're fuckin gutless.'

He's right, of course, I realise. I don't have the fuckin nerve.

He steps closer and I realise there's no malice in what he's about to do: I've threatened his life, and he just can't permit that. And so, he's going to stamp on my face again and again and again –

He comes a step closer, and I've got three seconds left to live and I'm trying to think of some oh so fucking clever line that's going to humiliate this bastard for ever and follow him for the rest of his life and make up for me and make up for Pete –

But as he reaches out to take the bottle from me all I can think of to scream is:

'You've got no fuckin friends, you bastard, everyone pretends to be friends with you cause they're fucking scared of you –'

His face creases, into –

– a smile –

– and I just don't have the nerve – and he knows it, he knows me, and I don't have the nerve, and the bottle slips under his chin –

The first point slips into his soft, jowelly throat and I just don't have the nerve –

The glass edge finds a vital artery and blood shoots out all over us, and I'm just a gutless little shitehawk, that's all I am –

And he falls on to his knees and on to the pavement, scrabbling at the flaps in his throat, hissing and gurgling away, and I kneel, and reach out – but I don't have the nerve to do it, I don't have the nerve to actually lay a finger on him –

And so carefully, carefully, so as not to touch his actual skin, I pull the van keys from his hand.

I get into his crappy Escort van. I fire it up and pull a U-turn and drive. And as I'm pushing the pedal as far as it will go I look in the mirror and just catch sight of a figure that might be Mary, gathering him into her arms, screaming and shrieking but then –

– as she pulls his face close to hers, their eyes meet and it seems for a moment like the terror fades from his face and the horror fades from hers and they're both there caught in each other's gaze, and caught in that moment, and in that moment there's no room for horror or terror, only space for something else; in the space where horror and terror should be there's just a vacuum, and because nature abhors a vacuum some new thing is created to fill the gap between them; and I try to give it a name because there is a word for it, I'm sure; but the word won't come to me now, the word was never there, and as the van pulls away I'm already forgetting them, forgetting that town and that life, and forgetting the hope that a word might bridge the gap between us.

The Shadow of a Boy

This play is for
Jan Morgan
David Owen
Peter Morgan
and for my nanna, Teresa Hughes

Acknowledgements

My thanks to Alison Hindell, David Britton, Sally Baker and all at Ty Newydd; to Jack Bradley, Sue Higginson, David Eldridge, Paul Miller and the National Theatre Studio; to Michael McCoy; to Andrea Smith and Andy Sperling for giving me a place to stay. And thanks to all at Paines Plough, for trips to the seaside and general hand-holding. *A diolch i Gareth Potter, o'r diwedd*

The Shadow of a Boy was first performed at the Loft, National Theatre, London, on 17 June 2002. The cast was as follows:

Luke	Rob Storr
Katie	Catrin Rhys
Nanna	Lynn Hunter
Shadow	Jo Stone-Fewings

Directed by Erica Whyman
Designed by Soutra Gilmour
Lighting by Steve Barnett
Sound by Rich Walsh

Scene One

Luke And so, it is with great regret I make my recommendation to the Star Council: the Planet Earth is not fit to join the Glactic League of Civilisations.
(*Deep voice.*) Agent 7272, do you recommend that the Planet Earth be scheduled for destruction, to preserve the Glactic Peace?
(*He considers: then, normal voice.*) No.
No. I believe there is hope for them.
They may one day be ready for Contact with the Civilised Universe.
(*Deep voice.*) Agent 7272, your mission is complete. Prepare for transport back to Glactic Centre /
(**Luke** *interrupts himself – normal voice.*) / No!
I'm not going back.
There is hope for the People of the Earth, but they need help. They'll never make it alone. I'm going to stay and do – whatever I can.
(*Deep breathing from the deep voice, then:*) Agent 7272, do you realise you are breaking every rule in the Contact rulebook?
(*Normal voice.*)
I realise that, sir.
Just tell my mum I love her and tell my dad –
(*Deep voice.*)
Tell him what, Agent?
(*Normal voice.*) – tell him I hope one day . . . he'll be proud of me.
(*Pause from the deep voice, then:*) I'm proud of you now, son. I'm proud of you now . . .
(*Normal voice.*) Goodbye, sir.

Luke *salutes.*

Katie Oh my bastard Christ.
They are gonna make mincemeat of you.

Beat.

Luke Who is?

Katie   Everyone.
Everyone in the comp is.
It's bad enough being a gyppo.
But – being a spaz that talks to himself as well.

Luke   I'm not a spaz that / talks to himself.

Katie   Don't even bother 'cause I just heard you. Talking to yourself. Like a spaz.

Beat.

Luke   I'm not a gyppo, though.

Katie   You are.

Luke   I'm not.

Katie   You are: Arthur Morris says.

Beat.

Luke   I'm not.

Katie   Oh.
All right then.
Fair do's.
(Beat.) I'll tell him you want a fight then, shall I?

Luke *looks at her.*

Katie   I'll tell him you wanna fight him for calling you a gyppo, shall I?

Luke *doesn't answer.*

Katie   Up in the woods at the back of the base he has them, straight after school finishes.
Straight after *comp* finishes, not after baby school finishes.
So you'll have plenty of time to get up there and shit yourself.
You're supposed to bring somebody to hold your coat and bag and stuff. But just – don't bring a coat is best, 'cause no one's gonna hold yours, are they?

Luke   Don't tell Arthur I wanna fight.

Katie   Why not?

Luke (*beat*)   'Cause – I don't mind.
I don't mind him calling me a gyppo.

Katie   You don't?

Luke   The thing is /

Katie   'Cause I bloody would. I bloody would mind that.

Luke   It's just – I'm not, am I?
I'm not a gyppo, so I don't mind him calling me one.

Katie   So – I can call you anything I like.
The nastiest thing I can think of.
And it's a lie. And it's not even true.
I can say the nastiest lie I like about you, and you don't
mind.

Luke *can't answer.*

Katie   So I could call you . . .
(*Searches for an insult: but changes her mind.*) Fair enough.
But if you're saying you're not a gyppo, Arthur's gonna
wanna fight you for calling him a liar.

Luke   I'm not calling him a liar. I'd never do that.

Katie   So you are a gyppo then?

Luke   No.

Katie   You just called Arthur Morris a liar: I'm gonna go
and tell him right now.

She spins on her heels.

Luke   No!
Don't.
Please.

Katie   Why not?

Luke   He's twelve. He's bigger than me.

Katie   What'll you give me if I don't tell him?

Luke   I –

Katie   I won't tell him – if you let me see your knickers.

Luke *hesitates.* **Katie** *holds his gaze. Finally,* **Luke** *begins to unbuckle his belt.*

Katie   Oh my God – you were gonna and all!

Luke   No I wasn't.

Katie   You bloody were, you were gonna whip your trousers down for me to see your knickers.

Luke   No!

Katie   Don't lie, you were.
I am gonna have so much fun with you.

Luke *looks at her.*

Katie   That's right.
I said: I am gonna have so much fun with you.
Do you wanna know how come?

Luke *nods.*

Katie   'Cause I'm your sister.
(*Beat.*) Go on, say something thick like, I can't be your sister
'cause you haven't got a sister. You know you want to.
(*Beat.*) I am gonna be
Your *school sister.*
And next year. In the comp.
You are going to be my little brother.
To guide and protect
And do with as I please.

Scene Two

Nanna *watches* **Luke***. Then:*

Nanna   What is it?

Luke *looks at her.*

Nanna *looks back at him.*

Luke *looks back at her.*

Beat.

Nanna   Fine.
We'll just sit here.
And wait.
(*Beat.*) I don't mind.
(*Beat.*) Take as long as you like.

Beat.

Luke *goes to speak.*

Nanna   Finally.

Luke *hesitates.*

Nanna *looks.*

Luke   What's . . . a gyppo, Nanna?

Nanna   Why d'you want to know that?

Luke (*beat*)   I wanna know . . . all sorts of things.

Nanna   Where did you hear that word?

Luke   I just . . . heard it. (*Looks.*)

Nanna   The word . . . echoed down the hillside, did it?
And you thought to yourself: oh, I wonder what that means.

Luke   Katie Fletcher /

Nanna   Oh here we go . . . /

Luke   Katie Fletcher said Arthur Morris said I was a
gyppo.

Nanna   Did she and did he?

Luke   And – I said I wasn't.

Nanna   Even though you don't know what one is?

Beat.

Luke   Well.
I don't . . . feel like I'm a gyppo.
Do you know what I mean?

Nanna   I should hope I do.
(*Beat.*) Good instincts, you see. Good instincts you've got.
There's this whole wide world out there
And there's always more of it than you can know
But so long as you've got good instincts
You're not going to go far wrong.
(*Beat.*) So long as you've got good instincts . . .
(*She waits.*)

Luke   . . . and you remember to say your prayers.

Nanna   Well, exactly.

They smile at each other.

Nanna   The thing to keep in mind with Katie Fletcher.
(*Beat.*) It's her mother.
I remember calling at their house to collect for the harvest
festival. And she'd –
– been to the bakers *and bought a sponge.*
A Victoria sponge.
I said to her, Mrs Fletcher – because I think she still is a
Mrs, in the eyes of the law at least – Mrs Fletcher, there's no
need to go to the bakers for sponge. You should've said, I'd
have given you my recipe for bara brith.
Oh no, she says, I'm a dead loss at baking. Nonsense, I say
to her, bara brith, it's the simplest thing you could imagine
and my recipe – well, my grandmother's recipe, to be exact
– my recipe is *simpler still.*
Even so, she goes, I'm sure I'd manage to make a mess of it
somehow.
Well, I said to her. I can hardly credit it.
A woman like yourself. A woman with education.
And oh, she goes, oh I'm afraid an education doesn't
guarantee expertise in the kitchen –
– well there's a thing, I tell her: a woman like yourself who
can't even make a bara brith for the harvest festival –

– and *still* you think you know better than the God that
made the sun and the sky and the stars and you won't send
little Katie to Sunday School.
(*Beat.*) That's what you're contending with.
When you contend with the Fletchers.
So my advice is just: steer clear.

Luke *is still worried.*

Nanna   What, lovely?

Luke   But Nanna –
– I still don't know –
What is a gyppo, then?

Nanna   Gyppo is a word that ignorant people – like Katie
Fletcher – call gypsies, or anyone who's a bit common, and
looks like they might steal clothes off the line.

Luke   So I am a gyppo, aren't I?

Nanna *looks.*

Luke   'Cause gypsies live in caravans, don't they.
And –
– I used to live in a caravan.

Nanna (*beat*)   You did.
You did, but you don't now.
(*Beat.*) Just – steer clear of her sort, is my advice.

Beat.

Luke   Well good.
I will steer clear.
I don't like her.

Nanna   It's not her fault, mind.

Luke   No, but I'm glad.
'Cause she was saying.

Nanna *looks.*

Luke   She was saying.

Nanna   *What*, lovely?

Luke   She was saying all this stuff about.
You know.
Her being my sister.
Like my school sister.
And she says I'm supposed to go round hers and have tea so she can tell me all about the comp, and then on the first day of school she's gotta sit with me on the bus and take me to my class and all that.
But I'm glad.
I'm glad I've gotta steer clear.
'Cause I don't wanna go round hers for tea and sit next to her on the bus –

Nanna   – Luke.

Luke *looks.*

Nanna   Why didn't you say straight off?

Luke   First things first you always say.
Or I've heard you say it sometimes.
And first, I wanted to know what a gyppo was and if I am one.

Nanna   I'm sure you did.
But you also wanted –
– you are sly as a snake.

Beat.

Luke   No.

Nanna   Luke –

Luke   Nanna –

Beat.

Luke   You said steer clear /

Nanna   I know.
(*Beat.*) It wouldn't be very nice if you got lost on your first day, would it.

Luke *says nothing.*

Nanna   Think what the teachers would say if you got lost and you were late on your very first day.

Luke *says nothing.*

Nanna   That wouldn't be a very good start, would it.

Luke   You said.
You said Katie was a bad apple.

Nanna   Well, she is, but I'm not telling you to pick up her bad habits /

Luke   And you said her mum was a right slack Alice.

Nanna   I said no such thing.

Luke   You did.
You did. You said it to Mrs Hughes.
You didn't say it, you spelled it out.
But I'm not five. I'm ten.
(*Beat.*) We were buying spuds at Jack Williams.
You talked for ages. You said we were going straight to the paper shop for my comic but then we popped into Jack Williams for spuds and there was / Mrs Hughes

Nanna   You –
– shouldn't have been listening.

Luke   I wasn't listening.
I just – heard.

Nanna *looks at him.*

Luke   She can't cook or anything.
I'll get food poisoning if I go for tea at theirs.
I'll die.

Nanna   There must be things you're wondering about the grammar school, things I don't know about.

Luke   There's not. There's nothing.
(*Beat.*) And it's a comprehensive, not a grammar school.

Nanna   Well –
– well, there you go, don't you?
I don't even properly know what it's called.

Beat.

Luke   Nanna.
I don't want to.

Nanna *looks at him.*

Scene Three

Luke   My nanna says I can't come over for tea on
Sunday, 'cause I have to go to Sunday School.

Katie   My mum says Sunday School's a load of rubbish,
but she understands how your nan would want a few hours'
peace from your whining over the weekend.

Beat.

Luke   So Nanna thought Saturday –

Katie   – Saturday's no good, Mum's working Saturday –

Luke   – which is why Nanna thought you could come
over to ours for tea on Saturday.
(*Beat.*) There's rhubarb coming up in the garden. We're
having proper home-baked rhubarb crumble.

Katie   I don't like proper home-baked rhubarb crumble.

Luke   How would you know? Your mum can't bake
nothing.

Beat.

Katie   D'you know what my mum says about your nan?

Luke   I don't care what any slack Alice says.

Beat.

Katie   She says your nanna
Has got a heart of gold.
(*Beat*). Which is what she always says when she thinks
someone's a mad old cow.

Beat.

Luke   I don't want you to come to ours.
Nanna says /

Katie   I'm sure you don't.
I wouldn't want anyone to come to mine if I lived in a dump
like yours.
But it'll be great.
I'll be able to see all your teddy bears, and dolls.
And find out how bad your house smells.
They usually smell.
Houses with old people living in them.
'Cause old people are nearly dead.
And dead things usually smell.
They usually smell like /
/ you're not going to cry, are you, Lukey?

Luke   No.

Katie   No?

Luke   I haven't got teddy bears and the house doesn't
smell.

Katie   Oh, and so you don't mind.
'Cause you don't mind people saying things that aren't true.

Luke *says nothing.*

Katie   What if I said something that is true, then?
(*Beat.*) What if I said –
– little orphan boy.
Haven't got no mummy.
Haven't got no dad.
It's one thing just having no mum. Or just having no dad. I
haven't got a dad. Loads of people haven't got a dad.
But having no mum *and* having no dad.

(*Beat.*) Talks to himself 'cause he hasn't got a mum or a dad to talk to.
Just a batty old nan.
Haven't got no mum.
Haven't got no dad.
That's – what they'll all be singing.
When you get on the bus the first day at school.
Here's the little freakboy
Who lives with his batty old nan.
(*Beat.*) They'll be saying – what was the last thing that went through Luke's dad's head?
Luke's *mum*.
(*Beat.*) And of course you'd crash your car.
Of course you would
If your son was a freak
Just to get some peace from his bloody whining.
(*Beat.*) Of course you'd crash your car.
Rather than go to parents' evening and schoolplay and sportsday and have to tell everyone yes, that's him, that's our son freakboy Luke blabbering away to himself in the corner. (*Beat.*) You gonna cry now, Lukey?

Beat.

Luke   No.

Beat.

Katie *goes to say something else.*
She stops herself.
Comes closer to **Luke** *and inspects him.*
She stares at him for a long time.

Luke (*looks at her, then*)   I'm not gonna cry.
'Cause I haven't got nothing to cry about.
(*Beat.*) I'm going now.

Beat.

Katie   Luke.

Beat.

Katie If someone.
At the comp, no one does stuff like showing their knickers,
right. That's just for baby school.
If someone asks you to show them your knickers, you do
this –

*She hooks the top of her pants with her middle finger and pulls them out
from her jeans: then she lets them slip back into her jeans, and presents
her finger.*

Katie – and you tell them to spin, all right?

Beat.

Katie Well, go on then. Show me.

Beat.

Luke *doesn't move.*

Katie Don't say I didn't try to help you, all right?

Luke *turns to go.*
He pauses.

Luke Katie?

Katie *looks.*

He gives her the finger.

Luke Spin on that.

Scene Four

Nanna *(beat)* You can say now, or I'll just have to sit here.
(She waits for him to speak. He doesn't.) If I don't get to bed soon,
I'm going to be awfully bad-tempered in the morning, and I
won't be in the mood to make porridge, and we'll end up
having the brussel sprouts from supper for breakfast /

Luke Katie was teasing me.

Nanna What about, lovely?

Luke *doesn't answer.*

Nanna *holds his gaze.*

Luke   She was trying to make me cry.

Nanna   You know what you have to do when someone says nasty things to try and upset you. You just have to think: are any of these things true?
And you'll find they're not true of you, but they might well be true of the person who's teasing you /

Luke   She –

Nanna *pulls up.*

Luke   She wasn't saying nasty things that aren't true. She was trying to make me cry.

Nanna (*beat*)   And did you?

Luke *shakes his head.*

Nanna   Good lad.

She gets quickly up.

Luke   Nanna?

Nanna *waits.*

Luke (*beat*)   Could you.
Can I have a story?

Nanna *doesn't answer.*

Luke   Nanna?

Nanna   Don't you think you're a bit old for stories? Wouldn't you rather read your comics?

Luke (*beat*)   S'pose.

Nanna *makes to go.*

Luke   Nanna.

Nanna *waits.*

Luke   I didn't cry.

Nanna   'Cause you're a good lad.

Luke   Katie asked me why I didn't cry.

Beat.

Can I have the story, Nanna?

Beat.

Nanna *turns, sits down again.*

Nanna (*beat*)   You'd stayed over with me, 'cause Mummy and Daddy were working late, building your house so you wouldn't have to live in the caravan.
When I woke it was raining, just a drizzle, but enough for the sunlight to catch and flicker in the drops, enough that there were tiny rainbows wherever you looked.
The light must've woken you.
Not the rain. The rain was too soft. It must've been the light.
(*Beat.*) I opened my eyes.
I breathed in.
I sat up.
And all round me were snowdrops.
Still damp from the garden. That fresh smell of the morning filling my bedroom.
(*Beat.*) The light had woken you.
The snowdrops had come up overnight and you'd put on your raincoat and your wellies and gone out into the garden and picked them.
And then laid them out around me, while I was still asleep.
(*Beat.*) Luke.

Luke   I was six, wasn't I.

Nanna   Yes, you were.
Luke –

Luke   I was just six, and I'd gone out and picked the snowdrops and that's how you knew it was –

Nanna (*beat*)   A special day.

Luke   A very special day.

Nanna (*beat*)   Your daddy was working for Mr Badham.
And your mummy was working at the Cartwheel.
And even when he was working very very late
Your daddy would stop by and look in on you.
You'd always try and stay awake.
You'd lie on your belly, propped on your elbows, your
fingers pushing your eyelids up so you wouldn't fall asleep.
You always did fall asleep in the end.
But your daddy stopped by and checked on you anyway.
(*Beat.*) The house was almost finished.
Your daddy had picked up your mum.
And God must've seen your house and seen how well your
daddy had built it.
And He thought He needed someone to build houses in
Heaven.
Because sometimes God picks people for special jobs.

Luke   Like the shepherds on the hillside?

Nanna   Like the shepherds on the hillside, that He sent to
greet the Lord Jesus.
(*Beat.*) Only the very best people.
And you're very lucky your dad was picked for such a
special job.

Luke   I know.

Nanna   And your mummy had to go with your dad –

Luke   – because how could Dad build houses without
Mummy to help him?

Nanna   Exactly.

Luke   And I never cried.
I never cried once.

Nanna   Not once.

Luke   And why not?
Why didn't I cry?

Nanna (*beat*)   What is there to cry about, when your
mummy and daddy are picked to do the Lord's work?

Luke   Nothing.

Nanna   Nothing.
(*Beat.*) I looked out over the garden and there wasn't a single
snowdrop to be seen. I thought you'd picked them all – but
you'd left one last patch: you'd hidden them.
You'd put a bucket over them to keep them safe. You didn't
realise they needed the rain and the sun, so they'd grow up
big and strong.

Luke   I know now, though.

Nanna   Yes, you do.

Luke   But Nanna –

Nanna *waits.*

Luke   – if Mum had to go with Dad, how come –

Nanna   Luke, please.

Luke   It's just, I don't quite understand /

Nanna *draws back from him: he dries up.*

Luke (*beat*)   Nanna –

Nanna (*turns back to him*)   – What now, lovely?

Beat.

Shadow   Luke.

Luke *doesn't respond.*

Nanna   Little man?

Shadow   Luke.

Nanna   It's better out than in, whatever it is.

Shadow   Luke.
You know why you had to stay behind.
Don't you.

Luke *looks at him.*

Shadow   Don't you.

Luke *doesn't answer.*

Shadow   You had to stay, 'cause you had a mission.
Right?
(*Beat.*)   Am I right?
(*Beat.*) Shadow to Luke, are you reading me, Luke?

Luke *barely nods.*

Shadow   At *last.*

Nanna   What is it, lovely?

Shadow   Could you get rid of her? We've got loads to do
and really – not that much time at all.

Luke (*beat*)   Nothing, Nanna.
I was just –

Nanna *looks at him.*

Luke   Can I read my comics for a bit, Nanna?

Nanna   It's already / well past your bed time.

Shadow   / I wonder what'd happen
If you were to look really really sad, right now.
Go on, give us a pout.

Luke *does so.*

Nanna (*beat*)   All right then. Just for a little while.

Luke   Thank you, Nanna.

Nanna *kisses him: leaves.*

Shadow (*watches her go, then*)   Star Cadet Luke: welcome to
the team.

Scene Five

Shadow's *weighed down with bits of kit dangling from straps and harnesses: in particular, he's hulking around a portable reel-to-reel tape recorder with a microphone dangling from it, and an early eighties model Polaroid. He snaps things occasionally, or inspects them with a plastic* Star Trek-*style tricorder.*

Shadow   And you use these for . . . what?

Luke   They're just flowers.

Shadow   Varieties of powderized wheat grain used in the making of bread?

Luke   They just look nice. And smell nice.

Shadow *sniffs sceptically.*

Shadow   Perhaps – to deeply primitive sense organs.

Shadow *fiddles with his Polaroid. It doesn't seem to be working.*

Oh, what now?

Luke   What's wrong?

Shadow   The . . .

Luke   Holographic scanner?

Shadow   The holographic scanner's playing up again.

He gives up on the Polaroid.

Luke   Was it like a rocket you came in? Or a saucer?

Shadow   Nothing like that. I didn't come in a *thing*.

Luke   They beamed you down?

Shadow   You might call it that. If you didn't know what you were talking about, at all.

Shadow *shakes himself down.*

Luke   What?

Shadow   This *body*. It's like it thinks there's only four dimensions in the universe.

Luke   Aren't there?

Shadow *looks at him.*

Luke   You'll need the names of them. The flowers.

Shadow   Really?

Luke   Of course.

Shadow   All right. If we must . . .

Luke   This is a bluebell, and this is a / primrose

Shadow   Hold on, hold on.

He struggles with the tape machine. **Luke** *watches.* **Shadow** *finally switches the tape on and holds the mike at* **Luke**.

Shadow   OK.

Luke   Right, so this is a bluebell, and this is a primrose, and this is forget-me-not, and these . . . these are just kinds of grasses. Nanna's got a book, I can look them up and find out exactly what kinds later /

Shadow   Can't I say they're just grass?

Luke   You can if you don't mind not doing your job properly.

Beat.

Shadow   We'll get the book. And what's this?

Luke   A foxglove.

Shadow   A glove for foxes? How does that work? How's a fox get that on his / paw?

Luke   No, that's just the name of it. It's not really a glove. And – don't touch them. They're poisonous. To humans, anyway.

Shadow   I'll keep that in mind.

Luke   And these are – ow!

Shadow   What?

Luke *rubs his hand.*

Luke   A stinging nettle.

Shadow   And what's that do?

Luke   Well it stings, doesn't it.

Shadow   Are you . . . gonna cry?

Luke   No.

Shadow   Does stinging not hurt then?
I thought stinging was a thing that hurt.
Does it not? Can you explain that to me somehow?

Luke   I'm not gonna cry.

Shadow (*beat*)   It's not very kind, is it, leaving stuff like
that around the place? Stuff that poisons you, stuff that
stings you. I'm not sure he's all you crack him up to be . . .

Luke *searches; finds what he's looking for.*

Luke   See this?
It's a dock leaf. It takes away the sting of the nettle thief.
And wherever you find stinging nettles, you find dock leaves
growing just by to make you better.

Beat.

Shadow   So . . . when do I get to meet him, then?

Luke   You can't *meet* Him.

Shadow   But it's the first thing I'm supposed to do. Hit
the ground, preferably running, collar some natives and
demand they take me to their leader, who you claim to be
this – (*He consults a notebook.*) – 'God' bloke.

Luke   Yeah, but you can't just meet Him.

Shadow   So what, do I . . . make an appointment?

Luke   No it's not like that, it's . . . You can't see Him, is the thing. You just know He's here.

Shadow   You just know.

Luke   You look around, and you just know.

Shadow   You look around at the stinging nettles and poison flowers?

Luke   You look around at the dock leaves and the pretty flowers.

Beat.

Shadow   Has he got a deputy or something I could talk to?

Luke   *No!*
Well, He's got vicars, and things.
I mean, there's my Nanna –

Nanna   Luke?

Luke   – but she's not really a deputy or anything. Not officially, like.

Nanna *comes into the garden.*

Nanna   Come in and wash your hands for tea.

Luke *pouts.*

Nanna   And then you can fetch the cheese and the salmon spread from the pantry.

Luke *pouts even more.*

Nanna   Fish is good for you, Luke.

Luke   Be better for you if it didn't have all bones in it.

Nanna   There's no bones in salmon spread.
Besides which, the Lord only puts bones in fishes so you'll take time over your food, instead of wolfing it down like a . . .

Luke   . . . wolf?

Nanna (*smiling*)   Just get in here and wash your hands, little man.

Nanna *leaves.*

Shadow's *staring at* **Luke**, *confused.*

Luke   What now?

Shadow   Just remind me again: fish?

Luke   What good are you?

Shadow   Well . . . there's a lot to take in, isn't there.

Luke   OK. Fishes are the things that live in the water –

Shadow   – oh yeah, and if you take them out of the water and put them on the land where we are, they die. (*Stares at him, then:*) They're things from the river?

Luke   Yeah.

Shadow   Those blue things you collect, the ones on your shelf?

Luke (*thinks; then*)   No! You idiot, those are bottles, mun.

Shadow   But you found them in the river /

Luke   Those are old bottles that people have thrown away, they're not living things.

Shadow   They're not living now, but how do you know they weren't alive before you pulled them out of the water?

Beat.

Luke   You are . . . the worst person I can think of for this job.

Shadow   Feeling guilty now, 'cause of all those bottles you killed /

Luke   You can't kill bottles, right? They're just . . . things. That people make. Fishes are *living* things. That God makes. And – they're just not the same . . . *kind* of thing.

Beat.

Though . . . once, I found a bottle in the river, and picked it up – and there was a fish inside it.

Shadow   What'd'you do?

Luke   I took it home. Put it on my shelf.

Shadow   And what happened?

Luke   The fish died.
Not straight away, like, but – after an hour or two.

Beat.

Shadow   So . . . do the fishes *live* in the bottles?

Luke   I don't know.
Maybe.
Anyway, there's no fish in the river any more.

Shadow   Where've they gone?

Luke   Uh . . . to the sea. I think.

Shadow   Maybe they haven't gone anywhere. Maybe it's part of the fish lifecycle, that after they've been fishes for a while they settle down and transform into bottles. Maybe the bottle is like a fish-chrysalis, and the fishes go into them for a bit and then come out as . . . seagulls. Or kingfishers. Or . . . butterflies.

Luke   I don't think so . . .

Shadow   And if the fishes do live in bottles, maybe that's why there's none in the river any more. 'Cause maybe collecting all the bottles from the river, you've . . . you've taken all the fishes' houses. And now they're just . . . wandering around the river, with nowhere to go, looking for their houses but they can't find them 'cause Luke has nicked them all and put them on his shelf. Did you ever think of that?

Beat.

Katie *approaches.*

Luke   Are you gonna be here long?

Shadow   Till my mission is completed. Or I die in the attempt.

Katie   All right, freakboy.

Luke (*beat*)   I wasn't talking to myself.

Katie   No. Well.
We both know you were.
(*Beat.*) Let's get this over with, shall we.

Katie *strides off.*

Shadow   What – was that?

Luke   That was – a girl.

Shadow   And what the hell are they?

Luke   They are –
– they're the same kind of thing as Nanna.

Shadow   Really?
'Cause that thing –

Luke   Katie Fletcher –

Shadow   – that Katie Fletcher didn't look anything like Nanna.

Luke   Katie's like eleven, and Nanna's . . . loads older than that.

Shadow   So they're at different stages of the lifecycle, are they?

Luke   . . . yeah . . .

Shadow   . . . and is there a chrysalis involved? Does a Katie go into a something and come out all different?

Luke (*beat*)   Yes.
Yes, there is.

There's a thing called *getting married.*
A Katie goes into that.
And when she's married she gets all wrinkly and old.
And she comes out – a Nanna.

Scene Six

Shadow   And pepper is?

Luke   It's just . . . to make food taste nice.

Shadow   Eating is a something we do so the body doesn't run out of energy.

Luke   I suppose . . . but you can make it taste nice as well.

Beat.

Shadow   And that's what all this . . . 'cookery' is about?

Luke   Yeah. There are people called chefs and that's all they do, is cook things really really well. And you go to their restaurants and dress up and have white wine or a pint of beer. And you have prawn cocktail to start, then chicken in a basket or spaghetti bolognese, and black forest gateau for sweet.

Shadow   It's the simplest thing, taking on fuel. Why d'you have to make it so fussy?

Luke   It's not fussy, it's good. Things don't have to be boring all the time.

Nanna (*coming in*)   Apparently at Katie's house they don't consider it important to wash hands before a meal.
I've shown her the sink and the soap and how the taps work. (*Beat.*) We'll just have to hope for the best.

Shadow   No, things don't *have* to be boring. They just are on this planet.

Luke   Don't moan 'cause you don't like it /

Shadow   Can you fly? 'Cause you can where I come from. Because we have transcended the brute corporeal existence you suffer in this dump.

Nanna   And I don't want to find any salmon spread sandwiches smeared across the bottom of the table, all right? 'Cause if I do, I'll scrape them off and fry them up and you'll be having them for supper.

Luke   I'll eat them properly this time, Nanna.

Shadow   Hold on –
– are you saying –
– all that fuss and you don't even like the stuff?

Luke   I don't like salmon spread sandwiches, no.

Shadow   So why d'you bother eating them?

Luke   'Cause Nanna says so.

Shadow   Chuck them to me, I'll dump them in the stream. Back where they belong.

Luke   No.

Shadow   She'll never find out.

Luke   That's not the point. She made it for me, and she said I got to eat it so /

Shadow   But you don't like it?

Luke   It's probably good for me.

Shadow   How can it be good for you if you hate it. That's rubbish.

Luke   I can see why they send you on all the really dangerous missions.

Shadow *looks at him.*

Luke (*beat*)   They send you on the dangerous missions 'cause you're the bravest and the best.

Shadow   I was only trying help you out.

Luke   I know /

Shadow   Just trying to help a mate, like.

Luke   I know /

Shadow   But if you don't want my help . . .

Luke   I do, though.

Shadow   Do you?

Luke *nods.*

Shadow   You sure?

Luke   Yes.

Beat.
In the distance, a siren.

Shadow   What's that then?

Beat.

Luke   Don't know.

Shadow   You've never heard it before.

Luke   I've –
– heard it before.
Just . . .

Shadow   You weren't really listening.

Luke   No.

Shadow   So. Now you are.
What is it?

Luke   I don't know.

Shadow   How you gonna find out?

Luke *looks at him.*

Shadow   Go on.

Beat.

Luke   Nanna?

Nanna   Mmmm?

Luke   What's that noise, Nanna?

Nanna   Just the pans rattling, lovely.

Luke   No, Nanna, like that wailing noise –

He does an impression of the siren.

Nanna   Why d'you want to know that, little man?

Luke *looks to* **Shadow**.
Shadow *whispers in his ear.*

Luke   'Cause . . . Katie said it was a signal for all the big kids at the comp, to stuff all the first years' heads down the toilet and flush it.

Nanna *relaxes.*

Nanna   It's a horn from the cheese factory in Whitland. It tells all the workers their shift is over.

Shadow*'s listening to this carefully – he looks to* **Luke***: Is this the truth?* **Luke** *picks up his glance.*

Luke   Really?

Nanna   Yes.

Luke   In Whitland? And the noise carries all the way to us?

Nanna   It has to be loud, lovely, so the workers can hear it over the machinery.

Luke *glances at* **Shadow***;* **Shadow** *shrugs.*

Luke   Fair enough, then.

Katie *enters.*

Nanna   Sit yourself down, Katie.
Would you like tea or coffee?

Katie   Tea.

Nanna   Good. Coffee, as we know, is the very nectar of the devil himself.

Nanna *holds* **Katie***'s gaze.*

Luke   Nanna thinks she's funny.

Nanna *cracks a smile.*

Nanna   Luke?

Luke *looks at* **Katie**, *then closes his eyes and clasps his hands.* **Nanna** *stares at* **Katie** *until she follows suit.*

Luke   Lord, we thank you for what we're about to receive, and pray that you bless us and preserve us. Amen.

Nanna   Amen.

Katie   A-men.

Shadow*'s peering at* **Katie**, *distracting* **Luke**.

Nanna   So, Katie, Luke's very eager to hear all about the comprehensive school. Aren't you, Luke?

Luke   Yes, Nanna.

Katie   What'd you wanna know?

Luke   Dunno. Anything, I s'pose.

Katie   All right then . . . Well . . . whatever you do, don't sit anywhere in the back four rows on the bus, or the sixth-formers'll kick you in.

Luke*'s getting alarmed 'cause* **Shadow** *has pulled out his Polaroid and is taking snaps of* **Katie**.

Luke   O-K . . .

Katie   And behind the metalwork block, there's some psycho kids have got their den there, and you see them going there every break and sniffing superglue and they come out with their eyes all like this – (*She flicks her eyes up into* *her head, so only the whites show.*) and all gunk around their mouths /

Nanna   Would you like some jam on your bread, Katie? I've got blackberry, and raspberry, and apricot. I made it myself, from the garden.

Katie   Have you got any strawberry?

Nanna (*beat*)   We have, but it's only rubbish from the shop, there's no proper fruit in it /

Katie   I'd much prefer strawberry, if that's all right with you.

Nanna *gets up and ferrets.*
Shadow *leans right in front of* **Katie** *to take a picture of her face.*
Luke *struggles not to look at him.*

Luke (*to* **Shadow**)   Will you get lost?

Shadow   All right, all right.

Shadow *scuttles away.* **Luke** *smiles nervily at* **Katie**.
Katie *stares back at him.*
Luke'*s smile dies.*
Satisfied, **Katie** *takes a mouthful of tea.*

Katie   God!

Nanna *spins round.*

Nanna   What?

Katie   Nothing. The tea's just really weak, is all.

Nanna   You've not burned yourself?

Katie *shakes her head.*

Nanna   Good. Here's your jam.

Katie *takes the jam without saying thank you, opens it up and starts ladling huge lumps of it on to her bread.*
Nanna *watches for a moment as* **Katie** *stuffs the jam-loaded bread into her mouth.* **Katie** *smiles at her.* **Nanna** *can take no more.*

Nanna　And I'd thank you not to use that sort of language while you're in my home.

Katie　I didn't say nothing.

Nanna　You blasphemed.

Katie *looks at* **Luke** *in bewilderment.*

Luke　You said (*He mouths.*) 'God'.

Katie　'God' isn't swearing. It *isn't.*

Nanna　It's not a rude word, no.

Katie　So what'd I do?

Beat.

I didn't do nothing, did I?

Beat.

Nanna　You know, Katie, just the other day, Luke had a jam sandwich, and he stuffed it in his mouth and dropped crumbs everywhere, and got jam all over his chops, and I said to him, 'Luke, you're as bad as Katie Fletcher.'

Katie *becomes horribly aware she's got jam on her mouth.*

Nanna　– and we had a little laugh about it. But I'd never say such a thing while you were here – that'd be rude. 'Cause that might well upset you, mightn't it.

Katie　Yes. It might well.

Nanna　And God is everywhere. So whenever you use the Lord's name to mean something bad, then you're going to upset Him.

Beat.

Katie　I think . . . I've had enough to eat now.

Beat.

Nanna　You don't want any rhubarb crumble?

Katie   No, thank you.

Nanna   But you've hardly had a thing /

Katie   I'm full, thank you very much.

Beat.

I'd like to go home now, please.

Nanna   You can't go home yet.
Your mother won't be back for another two hours.

Katie *says nothing.*

Shadow   You can't let her go yet. I've barely filled half a
. . . databank.

Luke   What am I supposed to do?

Shadow   You could – think of something?

Luke *(flusters, then)*   But you haven't seen my . . . collection
of old bottles, yet. From the river /

Katie   Oh well. That would be lovely. I'd love to see your
collection of old bottles, please Luke. And they're from the
river? That sounds . . . fascinating.

Beat.

Nanna   Well, in that case, you're both excused.

They get up and go to leave. **Luke** *leads the way.*
As **Katie***'s about to leave the room:*

Nanna   Katie.

Katie *stops.*

Nanna   If you do want something else to eat /

Katie   I'm sure I'll be fine, thank you very much, Mrs
Evans.

Scene Seven

Luke   These are the bottles.

Katie   Oh.
I don't know how you stick it.
(*Beat.*) All that God crap all the time.

She hovers at an immense, vast, huge pile of comics.

You like comics, do you?

Luke   A bit.

Katie   A bit?
My mum doesn't believe in comics. She says they promote neo-Fascist militarism.

Shadow *looks questioningly at* **Luke**. **Luke** *picks up the look.*

Luke   What's that mean?

Katie   They make boys think it's cool to shoot people.

Luke   Oh, I don't like them for the war stories.

Katie   No?

Luke   I like the – this is my favourite, 'Shadow of the Stars'. It's about this kid who – there's this thing, the Glactic League and they survey all the planets and decide if they're ready to join the League, and the Star Council send down this little alien called Shadow, and his mission is –

Shadow *stands to mock-attention, joins sarcastically in with* **Luke**.

Shadow/Luke   – 'to know and comprehend the people of the Earth, without prejudice or favour, to understand their virtues and their flaws, and to judge whether the Earth is ready to join the Glactic League of Civilisations'.

Shadow *salutes, goes back to peering at* **Katie**.

Shadow   And what a fantastic mission it's turning out to be . . .

Luke   – and no one on Earth can see Shadow except this
one boy, and the boy has to show Shadow around, and
explain stuff on Earth to him. I've got the whole story. It
starts in *Hawk* 34, the January 12th, 1978, issue, and ends in
Hawk 228, the Christmas issue in 1982.

Katie   And . . . what happens?

Luke   Well . . .
. . . loads of things.
But in the end, Shadow decides that the Earth isn't ready to
join the rest of Glactic civilisation –

Katie   – which any sane person can see in ten seconds –

Shadow   I like . . . girls' hair. Girls' hair is better than
boys' hair.

Luke   – but from learning about us, he decides that
Glactic civilisation is really boring, and so he wants to stay
here.

Katie   What a rem.

Shadow *looks at her.*

Katie   So, is this what you do?

Luke   What I . . . do?

Katie   You just read bollocks like that, and go to Sunday
School?

Luke   It's not . . .

Katie   It's not what?

Luke   It's not . . .
(*Beat.*) I think they're good, is all. I think it's a good story.

Katie   Why won't you say 'bollocks'?

Luke *doesn't answer.*

Beat.

Katie   I might sod off, I reckon . . .

Shadow *jabs* **Luke** *in the ribs.*

Luke   Do you want to . . . play a game?

Katie   What sort of game?

Luke   Uh . . . I've got Operation, and Ker-plunk, and Risk /

Katie   What about Nervous?

Luke (*beat*)   OK.

Katie   Tops. Come on then.

Luke   What'm I supposed to do?

Katie   You just come and sit down by me.
And what we do is, I put my hand on your knee –
– and you've gotta say if it makes you nervous.
Does it?

Luke (*beat*)   No.

Katie   So then I move my hand up a bit –
Does that make you nervous?

Luke   . . . No.

Katie   What about that /

Luke   Yes!

Katie *sniggers at him.*

Luke   That's a useless game.

Katie   And now you've got to do it to me.

Luke *hesitates.*

Katie   Or, I can tell everyone in comp you're a chicken . . .

Luke   All right, all right.

He complies.
She's wearing a skirt that falls a couple of inches above the knee when she sits.

Luke   Nervous?

Katie   No.

Luke *moves his hand a quarter of an inch up her leg.*

Luke   Nervous?

Katie   No.

Another quarter of an inch.

Luke   Ner/vous?

Katie   No.

Another quarter of an inch.

Luke   Nervous?

Katie   Not even slightly.

Luke*'s hand reaches the hem of her skirt. He slides his hand up another quarter of an inch – but over her skirt.*

Luke   Nerv/ous?

Katie   You're supposed to put your hand under my skirt.

Luke *stares at her for a second.*

Luke   I don't wanna play this any more.

Katie   You are *so* dead when you get to the comp.

Luke   I don't care.

Katie   But, you will.

She goes over to a window.

Luke   What're you doing?

Katie   Leaving. I reckon I can get on to your porch from here.

Shadow *looks to* **Luke**.

Luke   Your mum's not home yet.

Katie   Aw, that's right, I'd better sit round here for two hours with you boring me shitless then, hadn't I.

Shadow *looks carefully at* **Katie**, *then whispers to* **Luke**.

Luke   I'll tell you a secret if you stay.

Katie   Oh yeah?

Luke *nods.*

Katie   Do you even know any good secrets?

Luke   This one's really good.

Katie *sits down on the bed.*

Katie   Tell away, then.

Luke   If you get in the river where it comes through our garden, and walk down it back towards the village, you come to the hedge between Mr Scale's farm and Mr Beynon's farm. And that hedge – isn't a hedge. It's a stream, but it's all so overgrown it looks like a hedge.

Katie   That better not be it.

Luke   That's not even half of it. 'Cause if you walk up this stream, it's like crawling through the jungle, and you get your face scrammed to bits, but after you've got your face scrammed to bits you come out by this old bridge, on the backroad to Robinson Wathen.
When you're driving down the backroad, you've got to be lucky 'cause it's two and a half miles and only one ditch to overtake in, so if you meet someone coming the other way, you're in trouble. You've gotta reverse all the way back to where you came from.
But usually you don't meet anyone, 'cause no one knows about it, just people from the valley who cut through. And the only other people who go on that road are Arthur Morris, and Paul Barclay, and Davy Matthews and all those kids from the comp. They go down there and hang round on the bridge, and they chuck stuff in the stream, and try to fish with these little rods they made out of sticks.

And when they're sitting there pretending to fish . . . they
talk about girls.
They talk about what girls they like in the comp.
Paul Barclay likes Joanne Moore, and Davy Matthews likes
Mary Francis. Arthur Morris liked Gaynor Price, but now
he likes Anna Price. Cause, he says, Anna isn't so tight. And
I know, because I go there, after school.
And . . . I just sit. There's a couple of big rocks under there
sticking out of the water and I get there and sit with the
fishes and the moss and the spiders, and I hear . . .
everything.

Katie   That is a cool secret.

Luke   Yeah.

Katie   That is a fucking cool secret.

Luke *recoils a little at the oath.*

Katie   Have you ever said a swear word in your life?

Luke   Yeah.

Katie   Say 'fuck' then.

Luke *says nothing.*

Katie   Or 'bastard'.

Luke *says nothing.*

Katie   Or at least 'shit'.

Beat.

Why're you scared of saying stuff like that?

Luke   I'm not scared. I just . . . don't want to.

Katie   Is it 'cause it upsets your nanna?

Luke   Nuh.

Katie   Is it 'cause . . . it upsets God? Do you think you'll
burn in hell if you say a swear word?

Shadow   Is that true? Is that what he does to you?

Luke *(to both)*   No!

Shadow   What a bastard . . .

Katie   You are scared, aren't you?

Luke   No! I just don't wanna say them words, all right? I'd say them if I blummin well wanted to.

Katie   You 'blummin well' would, would you?

Luke   Yeah.

Katie *stares at him.*

Kate   Do you wanna know a secret, Luke?

Luke *doesn't know; glances to* **Shadow**.

Luke   What sort of secret?

Katie   The biggest secret in the world.

Luke   S'pose.

Katie   Are you sure? 'Cause you can't forget it once you know.

Beat.

Luke   Go on then.

Katie   Say 'shit'.

Luke   You didn't say I / had to –

Katie   Say 'shit' if you want to know the biggest secret in the whole wide world.

Luke   No.

Shadow   Luke!

Luke   No.

Shadow   Oh right, I'll just turn up at Glactic Centre and say 'Oh yeah, there's this really big secret on Earth –

Katie   Just once, Luke.

Shadow   – but I never quite managed to find it out.
Sorry, like.'

Katie   Did you know, Luke, 'shit' is Welsh for 'how'. So
you could make the sound, but just be saying 'how' in
Welsh.

Shadow   I think that's actually true.
(*Beat.*) It was in the Planetary Notes.

Katie   So it wouldn't really be swearing.

Beat.

Luke   OK then . . .
Shit.

Katie   I can't believe you swore.

Luke   It wasn't swearing, it was Welsh.

Katie   You don't speak Welsh.

Luke   No, but – I was saying 'how' in Welsh.

Katie   You said 'shit'. You're gonna burn in hell.

Luke *opens the window.*

Luke   You can go now, if you want.

Katie   Don't you want to know the secret?

Beat.

Luke   All right then.

Beat. **Katie** *smiles*

Katie   They're going to kill us all.

Luke *looks.*

Katie   They're gonna fry us. With great big bombs. And
even one bomb is enough to destroy the Earth, and they've

got hundreds and millions of them. And they're gonna blow us up.

Beat.

Luke   Why?

Katie   Nobody knows.

Luke   When?

Katie   They won't say. There'll just be a warning. It'll be on the telly. We'll get three minutes and then – boom. That's the end of everything.

Luke   But . . . we haven't got a telly.

Katie   You won't even get a warning then.

Luke   But that's / not fair.

Katie   You'll just be there one day having your tea and – there'll be this light and the house will fall down and you and your nanna'll be blown to bits.
(*Beat.*) But then again – do you hear the siren at nights sometimes?

Luke *nods.*

Katie   Do you know what it is?

Luke *shakes his head.*

Katie   It's from the base. It's where all the Americans keep their bombs. And that's their siren to say that they've got to blow them all up. So when you hear that, you know – boom. You're gonna get it.

Luke   But – I hear that every night, nearly.

Katie   They've got to test to make sure it's working properly.

Luke   So how do you know if they're testing it or if it's . . . for real?

Katie   If you hear it and three minutes later you're not blown to bits, then you know they were just testing it out.

Silence.

Fucking cool secret, huh?

Luke *nods.*

Scene Eight

Shadow *enters, stands right behind* **Luke** *with the Polaroid. He waits for* **Luke** *to turn round and snaps as he does so.* **Luke** *jumps.*

Shadow   Bit –
– jumpy, Luke?

Luke   'Course I am, with you creeping up behind me.

Shadow   Sorry. What you up to?

Luke   I think rabbits or something have been at the flowerbeds. Look, half the bluebells've been ripped up, and the primroses are all gone, / and

Shadow   Oh, that was me.

Luke   What?

Shadow   I was studying them, and I thought maybe I was starting to see what you meant, about them being pretty to look at and nice to smell. So I picked a couple. So I could have them with me to look at whenever I want.

Luke   You can't do that.

Shadow   No?

Luke   'Cause then they die. And then no one else can look at them.

Shadow   Oh. Sorry.

Beat.

Shadow   Making a bit of a nuisance of myself today, aren't I?

Luke   Yeah.

Beat.

Shadow   Still. You must be pleased.

Luke   What?

Shadow   You were crapping yourself about all that getting your head ducked down the toilet at the comp. Must be a weight off, not having to worry about that any more.

Luke *looks at him.*

Shadow   You know, if you're all gonna be . . . (*He draws his finger across his throat.*)

Beat.

Luke   You didn't believe all that, did you?

Shadow   Well, yeah.

Luke   You mong.

Shadow   Didn't you believe it?

Luke   Why would I believe anything Katie Fletcher says?

Shadow   You reckon she made it up?

Luke   Well, obviously.

Shadow   What'd she do that for?

Luke (*beat*)   She thinks it's funny trying to frighten people.

Shadow   Well, that's not very good.

Luke   Well I know. Don't worry though – God'll sort her out.

Shadow   Mmm.

Luke   What?

Shadow   It's just –
– there is the air base. Full of Americans.
And the siren.

Luke   That's from the cheese factory / in Whitland.

Shadow   In Whitland, I know.
I heard what Nanna said.
I was listening.

Luke *looks at him.*

Shadow (*beat*)   It's a long way, for the sound to carry.
It'd make more sense if it came from the base.

Beat.

Luke   Obviously the bits are all there, aren't they?
If you're gonna tell a lie, you use bits of real things that're
round you.
You take bits of real things and you put them together the
wrong way and – you've got a lie.
You have to do it like that, otherwise – it'd just be obvious
you were lying, wouldn't it?

Shadow   You sound like – a bit of an expert, Luke.
You do a lot of lying, then?

Luke   I never tell a lie.

Shadow   Hear a lot of them, do you?

Beat.

Luke   No.

Beat.

Shadow   All right.
All right then.
It's just.
The other reason I don't think she made it up is –
(*He hesitates:* **Luke** *waits.*) – we've seen it before.
On dozens of worlds.
They can't quite make the leap to the next level – so they

blow themselves to bits . . .

You wouldn't even see the explosion. There'd be a flicker of light, then the heat would burn your optic nerve away and everything would go dark.

The eighty per cent of you that is water would flash to steam. Your fat would take a fraction longer to evaporate: you might even feel it sizzle for a moment before it fell away from your skeleton.

Your muscles would char, and your bones would blacken and turn to powder, and when the blast wave hit you'd crumble and be carried up into the atmosphere, maybe right to the edge of space.

Most of the powder that was you would fall straight back to earth. If you fell on land, the land would be poisoned. If you fell on people, cancers would grow where you touched them.

But some of you would hover up in the sky for a while. You'd go sailing round the world, till finally gravity dragged you down. The last of you would flare and burn as you fell through the atmosphere, and maybe people on the ground would see you burn, and think you were a shooting star, and make a wish on you. And if they did, they would wish . . . to be dead.

(*Beat.*) All this, from splitting proton, from neutron, from electron.

The most basic structure.

Crack it, and out comes a force

That could consume you completely,

And leave just a shadow on the ground

To show where once a boy had been.

Shadow *steps close to him.*

Are you . . . going to cry, Luke?

He reaches out his hand to touch **Luke***'s cheek and feel for tears. Beat.*

Shadow   That's a relief then. You won't have to worry about the boys at the comp teasing you for being the last one to get hairs on your willy. 'Cause everybody's hair'll just be singed off, won't it.

Luke   Get lost.

Shadow   Only trying to look on the bright side.

He goes over to the flowerbed.

Actually, I think I will pull a few more of these flowers. I mean, I get what you're saying about leaving them for other people to see, but if they're just gonna get blown to bits I may as well take them back with me. Dry them. Put them in a museum.
'Cause we'll probably do that, we'll probably set up a museum about this place. Once you're all dead, like.

Katie *enters.*

Katie   My mum says I've gotta come and play with you for at least half an hour or there's no telly tonight.

Luke   Oh, lucky me.

Katie   Don't think I wanted to.

Luke   I don't.

Beat.

Katie   Is there any fish in this stream?

Luke   No.

Shadow   Yeah, and tell her why, Luke.

Katie *stares into the stream.*
Luke *stares at* **Katie**.
Eventually **Katie** *feels* **Luke**'s *gaze on the back of her head. She turns round.*

Katie   What?

Luke   You don't seem too bothered.

Katie   About what?

Luke   That we're all gonna be killed.

Katie (*beat*)   Everything dies, doesn't it.

Luke   Yeah, but . . .

Katie   But?

Beat.

Luke   Doesn't matter.

Shadow *watches* **Luke** *chicken out.*
He dumps his recorder, Polaroid, bits and bobs and walks over to
Luke *and grabs him in a headlock.*

Shadow (*to* **Katie**)   But you'll have to watch your mum
with her face all melted and her arms blown off, screaming
and begging you to give her some water but you can't 'cause
there's just these holes in her face, so you can't tell if you'd
be pouring the water down her mouth or into her nose or
into the spaces where her eyes used to be.

Luke *throws* **Shadow** *off.*

Katie   What'd you say that for?

Luke   I didn't say nothing!

Shadow   – and anyway all the water would be poison –

Katie *blocks her ears.*

Katie   I don't wanna hear –

Shadow   – and even if there was water that wasn't poison,
you couldn't get it, 'cause your whole body's burnt so
whenever you move it hurts so much you scream out you
wanna die and your mum loves you and she can't bear to
hear you screaming so she tries to clamp her hands over her
ears but she can't cause her arms've been blown off so in the
end all she can do is stand up and run against the wall and
batter her head till she knocks herself out.

Katie   That is *horrible* . . .

Luke   Hadn't you ever thought about it?

Beat.

Katie   Not . . . like that.

Luke   But you knew. You knew all this stuff.

Katie   Yeah, but I didn't –

Shadow (*to* **Katie**)   It's not hard to put it together. Once all the bits are in place.
(*Beat.*)
And you were calling me a rem.
You rem.

Katie   I just.
Didn't see it.

Shadow (*looks from* **Katie** *to* **Luke**)   Who'd want to see it? You and the being you love most in the universe; the both of you flayed; burned; dying.
I always wonder: does the screaming take over because the physical agony stops you speaking, or just because . . . there aren't the words.

Katie   I couldn't bear it, watching my mum die.

Shadow   You probably won't have to. Given an equal dosing of the old glow-in-the-dark rays, the kids tend to go first. The less your body mass, the less you can take. So probably it'll be your mum who gets to watch you die. And that way she'll see what's coming to her. Lots of parents say the watery vomiting is the most distressing stage, 'cause it's just like when their little baby had a tummy bug and they think . . . they can't help but delude themselves you're going to get better.
Until of course, your teeth start to fall out and your gums turn to mush and you start to bleed from everywhere /

Katie   Or if I went first. Knowing I was dying and my mum watching me and knowing what she was going through 'cause she couldn't help me.

Shadow *peers at* **Katie**.

Shadow   She's crying!

Luke   Katie.
Katie.
It's all right.

Katie   Why is it like this?

Luke   Look at me: am I afraid? Am I crying?

Katie *looks at him; shakes her head.*

Luke   I'm not.
'Cause there's nothing to cry about.
Everything that happens, even if it seems really bad, it's for the best.
'Cause that's the way God plans it.

Katie   Even this?

Luke   Even this.

Katie   How can this be for the best?

Luke   Well, it's like – like with the Good Samaritan, he wouldn't have had the chance to be good if the Syrian hadn't got beaten up by the robbers.
When bad things happen, it's to give us a chance to make things better.

Katie   When we're all burned and screaming and there's no one coming to save us?

Beat.
Luke *hasn't got an answer.* **Katie** *turns away.*

Luke   Katie, please don't cry /

Shadow   Nanna would know.

Luke *looks at him.*

Shadow   She'll understand it.
If anybody does.

Beat.

Luke (*to* **Katie**)   I'll ask my nanna. She's bound to understand.

Katie   D'you think so?

Luke   For definite.

Katie   What can she say?

Luke   I don't know. But – she'll explain it.

Katie   And you'll explain it to me?

Luke   And then you won't have to worry.

Shadow   About the blistering, and the bubbling /

Luke *silences him with a stare.*

Katie   I'd better go.
(*Beat.*) I'm scared to go home.
I'm scared in case it happens tonight. What if it happens tonight and we all get burned and my mum's crying 'cause she knows she's gonna have to watch me die – and I won't know what to say to stop her crying. I won't know what to tell her so she'll understand it's all OK.

Luke   It won't happen tonight, Katie, I promise you. I'll ask my nanna and she'll explain it to me and I'll tell you tomorrow and then it'll all be fine. And there'll be no reason to cry.

Beat.

Katie   All right then.

Katie *leaves.*

Shadow   Nicely done, Luke. I think you fooled her.

Luke   I didn't fool her about nothing.

Shadow   Oh no?

Luke   I'm gonna ask Nanna, and she's gonna explain it.

Shadow   You . . . actually think she will?

Luke   Of course.

Shadow   You think she'll have an explanation?

Luke   I know she will.

Shadow   Star Cadet Luke, you are bloody priceless. Glactic Centre are gonna piss themselves.

Scene Nine

Shadow *skulks, tape-recording the conversation.*

Nanna   I saw you playing with Katie this afternoon.

Luke   Was for a bit.

Nanna   She didn't – do anything?

Luke   No.

Nanna   So you're all right, then?

Luke   Yes.

Nanna   It's just you don't seem / like

Luke   I'm fine.

Beat.

Nanna   Well, now I know there's something wrong, don't I. You're such a good boy ordinarily, I don't know that I could say I know how it looks when you tell a lie, because I can hardly recall an occasion when you've lied to your nanna.
But I know how it looks when you're not happy.

Beat.

I'll just sit here, then, till you decide to tell me.

Luke   Nanna, it's –
– it's something awful, Nanna.

Nanna   We won't know that until we hear it.

Luke   I don't wanna say.

Nanna   Well –
– hold on. It's not Wednesday, is it?

Luke (*shakes his head*)   Why?

Nanna   Just the Lord Jesus left me a note saying that Wednesdays this month were going to be really busy for him, so on Wednesdays he wouldn't be able to help me sort out your problems.
But given that it isn't a Wednesday: do you really think there is anything that me and the Lord Jesus can't sort out between us?

Luke   No.

Nanna   No. Let's have it then, so I can be off to my bed.

Beat.

Shadow   Go on, then.

Beat.

Luke (*to* **Shadow**)   What if she hasn't got an answer?

Shadow   Of course she'll have an answer.

Luke   You think?

Shadow   For definite.
(*Beat.*) She'll make one up.
She'll tell you a story
To make you feel better.
(*Beat.*) She'll lie.

Beat.

Don't you think it'd be useful to know how it looks when your nanna lies to you?
Don't you think you should learn to read the signs?

Luke *can't answer.*

Shadow   You have to ask her.
You told Katie you would.
Nanna'll tell you a story, then you can tell it to Katie and
everything'll be fine again.

Nanna   Luke?

Beat.

Luke   All my bottles – I think I've driven the fish out of
the river.

Nanna *looks at him carefully.*

Luke   'Cause I've taken the bottles, now the fish have got
nowhere to live and so they've all gone /

Nanna   Is that what you're worried about?

Luke *nods.*

Shadow   Oh, I see: you don't need to learn
How it looks when your nanna lies to you.

Nanna   Oh, you daft little thing. Of course you haven't
driven the fish out of the river.

Shadow   You don't need to learn how it looks when your
nanna lies to you –

Nanna   That's all you were worried about?

Shadow   – because you learned that ages ago.

Luke   No.

Nanna   Well, what then?

Shadow   He wants to know why God's gonna let them
blow / up the world.

Luke   Shut up!

Luke *dives on* **Shadow**.
They wrestle.

Nanna   Luke! Luke!

Shadow *breaks free from* **Luke** *and runs away.*

Nanna   What on earth is wrong with you, lovely?

Luke *goes to speak.*
Changes his mind.
He picks himself up and dusts himself off.

Luke   It's nothing, Nanna.
I'm fine. Don't upset yourself.
It's nothing for you to worry about.

Scene Ten

Luke *sits up in bed in the dark.*
Shadow *sits at the other end of the bed with all his apparatus.*

Shadow   So – nervous?

Luke *shakes his head.*

Beat.

In the distance, a siren.

Shadow   Here we go . . .

Shadow *starts taking pictures of* **Luke**'s *face.*

Nervous yet, Luke?

Luke   No.

Shadow   The bombs are on their way, Luke.

Luke   The Lord wouldn't do that to us.

Shadow   Two minutes to go, matey boy.

Luke   I'm not listening . . .

Shadow *grabs his mike and thrusts it into his face.*

Shadow   Any last thoughts you'd like to share with
Glactic civilisation?

Luke   Rhubarb-rhubarb-rhubarb-rhubarb-rhubarb –

Shadow   What's that sound?

Luke   – rhubarb-rhubarb-rhubarb-rhubarb –

Shadow   I think I can actually hear the bombs whistling through the air.

Luke   Our Father which art in Heaven hallowed be Thy Name –

Shadow (*taking a snap*)   I'm gonna call that one 'A primitive biped wards off fusion bombs by means of ritual chant'. Unless you can think of something snappier?

Luke   – Thy Kingdom come, Thy Will be done –

Shadow   That's right, Lukey: His will be done. He wants this, He wants this to happen. He wants this to happen to you. He loves you *that much.*

Luke *pulls up.* **Shadow** *freezes, stares at him.*

Shadow   Well, bloody hell.

Shadow *peers forward. He reaches into his pockets, pulls out a cotton bud and a test tube.*
He leans forward and wipes the cotton bud under **Luke***'s eyes. He looks at the bud, then puts the bud into the test tube.*

Shadow   A tear, Luke.

He holds another bud ready. No further teardrops emerge.

One single, solitary tear.
Is that the best you can do?
'Cause it can get worse yet, Luke.
It can still get worse, if it has to.

Scene Eleven

Luke *and* **Katie** *are bouncing a beach ball between them.*
Shadow *comes into the garden with them.*

Luke   D'you know, the sky over the Preseli Mountains goes exactly the same colours every night.

Katie   I've decided where I want to be when it happens.

Luke   It goes red, but not like red sauce, more like rust; then it goes purple, like cherry Space Dust.

Katie   I want to be at school. At the comp. First, 'cause if I'm there, then Mum won't have to see me burned and crying.

Luke   Then purple turns to blue, the colour that Nanna calls navy blue, even though it isn't blue like pictures of the sea.

Katie   And, second, 'cause there's this basement below the metalwork block, and I don't think the caretakers know the lock is broken.

Luke   But maybe the sea is that colour blue, when you're in a submarine, miles under the water.

Katie   I'll show it you when you come to school. If you ever do.

Luke   Then it goes black, which is just like black.

Katie   And if I got down into the basement, I reckon I wouldn't take such a massive dose.

Luke   Then at about four in the morning, the black starts to turn back into blue.

Katie   So I'd live a bit longer, which would be awful, of course.

Luke   Then the blue fades to grey, then the sun comes and fries the grey red again. It's exactly the same, every night.
(*Beat.*) And I really wish it would change. Just some variety would be nice.

Katie   But at least I could come up and watch Davy Matthews and Paul Barclay and Arthur Morris and all those bastards die.

Luke *looks at her.*

Katie   What?

Luke   Nothing.

Katie   What?

Luke *grabs for the ball but knocks it away. He goes chasing after it.*

Shadow (*to* **Katie**)   It's just I heard them lot all talking about you the other day.

Luke *returns with the ball.*

Katie   When?

Luke *doesn't want to say.*

Katie   When'd you hear them?

Luke   The other day. I was under the bridge, and they were all talking about you.

Katie   What'd they say?

Luke *says nothing; bounces the ball back to her.*

Katie   They talk bollocks, you know. You can't believe a word they say.

She throws the ball to **Luke***;* **Shadow** *swoops in and intercepts.*

Shadow   Arthur Morris said he had three fingers up you Friday night.

He passes the ball back to **Katie***. She turns away.*

Luke   Paul Barclay said he was gonna have a go this Friday night.

Beat.

And he reckoned he was gonna get four.

Beat.

Four fingers. Up you.

Beat.

What does that mean, Katie?

Katie   It means /

Luke   'Cause I thought you didn't like them.
I thought you wanted to spend your last hours on earth
watching them die.

Katie   I wait for the siren. And when the siren comes, I
freeze up, and I sit there –

Luke   – waiting to be killed.

Katie   And I can't bear it. Not all the time.

Luke   I bear it.

Katie   And there's things you can do . . . that stop you
thinking about it. Just for a little while, just for a couple of
seconds.

Luke   And you do them with Arthur Morris.

Katie   And Paul Barclay and Davy Matthews and anyone.
Just to stop thinking about it.

Luke   With anyone?

Katie   Anyone.

Luke   With *anyone*?

Beat.

Katie   You'd say it would upset God.

Shadow   I don't think I care about that any more.

Luke   I don't think . . .
I want to play with you any more.

Shadow *slumps.*

Scene Twelve

Luke *and* **Nanna** *are at the table.* **Shadow** *watches.*

Luke   I hate liver and onions.

Nanna   That's a pity.
They're terribly fond of you.

Luke   Could I just eat the onions?

Nanna   'Course you can.

Luke   And then have bread and butter to fill up on?

Nanna   So long as you finish the liver before you start on
the onions.

Luke   That's not fair.

Nanna   Nor will you be, after I lock you in the coalshed.

Luke   You can try.

Nanna *looks up sharply.* **Luke** *can't hold her gaze.*

Nanna   I think you've been spending a bit too much time
in the company of Katie Fletcher.

Luke *prods miserably at his liver.*

Nanna   Just try to eat most of it. It'll help you grow up big
and strong.
Those boys at the comp won't be able to scare you then.

She gets on with her food.
Luke *stares at her for a beat. Then looks over at* **Shadow**.
Shadow *walks over to the table, picks up* **Luke**'s *plate, and very
deliberately drops it on the floor.*

Nanna   What in Heaven's name did you do that for?

Luke   I'm not scared of the comp boys. I'm gonna watch
them all die.

Nanna   You get to your room, now. Don't let me ever
hear you saying such things again.

Luke *starts towards his bedroom.*

Nanna   I'm at a loss with you, Luke Evans. I try my best
and it seems to go to nothing.
(*Beat.*) Just you go to bed, and pray, and think long and hard
about the way you're behaving lately.

She seems to have finished. **Luke** *starts again towards his room.*

You're family, and I'll always love you. But I don't think I
like you very much these days.

Luke (*beat*)   If you don't like me . . . why don't you get rid
of me?

Scene Thirteen

Katie *comes into the garden with some blankets.*
She sits down, arranges the blankets around her.
Luke's *sat up in bed,* **Shadow** *sitting at the far end.*

Shadow   Homes?
I don't get it. It's a new concept.

Luke   Where kids go. When their families can't cope with
them.

Shadow   What're they like?

Luke   Horrible.
But if you're in one of them, it means your family don't
have to watch you die.

Shadow   Right –
– smart.
So the families struggle with the kids for as long as they can
bear, then package them off to these . . . 'homes'.

Luke   Yeah.

Shadow   And can they have more kids then, if they want?

Luke   Well . . . I don't know.
I s'pose.

Shadow   Amazing.
You know, when I first got here, I looked around and I
thought – what the hell are all the grown-ups doing? All this
frantic activity, and when you figure it out, it's all for crap.
Back where I come from, we're exploring the galaxy and
figuring out the secrets of the universe and unearthing the
ruins of ancient civilisations and down here you're all –
rushing around and trying to scrape together the cash for a
Betamax. And it's all bollocks.
(*Beat.*) But this is a subtle planet.
It's not all how it seems on the surface. That stuff with the
food all the grown-ups do –

Luke   – cooking it, you mean?

Shadow   – yeah, and, arguing about what you watch on
the telly – what's that about? And *money*! All these little
tokens floating around, and all the energy that takes up,
worrying about paying the mortgage and worrying about
paying the rent, and worrying about the job, and worrying
about being on the dole.
But I just didn't see –
– the beauty of it all.
(*He looks at* **Luke**.) You know what it's really all about, don't
you?

Luke *shakes his head.*

Shadow   It's so they don't have to be like you.
They fill their heads up with all this crap
So they don't have to lie awake night after night
Waiting for the siren –

Luke   – waiting to be killed.

Shadow   Exactly!
And – oh, oh, this is incredible! – and *that's* why they have
kids at all – to give themselves more to get worked up about.
So they get to stamp around downstairs fuming about being

at the end of their tether and where did they go wrong and
what they hell are they going to do –
– while you lie awake in bed, shitting yourselves: so they
don't have to.

Beat.

Why didn't you tell me that's all you kids were for?
I wouldn't have wasted my time, I'd've gone straight to a
grown-up.
(*Beat: he studies* **Luke**.) 'Cause . . . you did understand that,
didn't you, Luke?
I mean, you must've put all the pieces together.
A bright boy like you.

Luke *gets out of bed.*

Shadow   What you doing?

Luke   Katie said you could climb down the porch roof
from my window.

Luke *goes over to* **Katie** *in the garden.* **Shadow** *comes over and
watches.*

Katie   I thought you were never coming.

Luke *doesn't answer.*

Katie   D'you wanna get under here?

She holds open the blanket for him. He doesn't move.

Luke   The siren's late tonight, isn't it?

Katie   D'you think that means anything?

Luke (*beat*)   They might not test it if they knew they were
gonna have to use it for real later.

Katie   Don't say that /

Luke   Arthur Morris, though. He's horrible.

Katie   I know.

Luke   When Arthur Morris was in our school, he never used to wash his hands after he'd been to toilet. He used to chase people around, saying he had all . . . poo on his hands. If he caught you he'd wipe his hands in your face and say you had his poo on your face. He'd stick his fingers in your mouth and say you were eating his poo /

Katie   I can't remember the last time I slept, Luke.

Luke   Me neither.

Katie   If you came under here with me, maybe we'd be able to.

Luke   I don't think Nanna'd like it.

Katie   No.

Luke   I don't think God'd be very happy with me, neither.

Katie   I don't s'pose he would, no.

Katie *holds open the blanket.*
Shadow *watches.*
In the bedroom: **Nanna** *enters and sees the empty bed.*
In the distance, the siren goes.
Luke *and* **Katie** *stare at one another.*

Katie   Luke. Will you – (*Reaches out to him.*)

Nanna   Oh, God, please, let him come back to me –

Shadow *spots* **Nanna**.
He walks back to the bedroom.

Nanna   – I know it's a sin to test You, Lord, but please just bring him back safe to me –

Shadow *stands and watches her.*
The siren falls silent.
Nanna *listens intently.*

Katie   Luke – if we don't go straight away – you won't leave me, will you?

Luke   Of course not.

Katie   D'you promise?

Luke *says nothing.*

Katie   If this is it, and we're burned, you won't leave me?

Luke   I promise.

Katie   You won't leave me, hurt and on my own?

Luke   I won't.

Katie   You won't let me die alone?

Luke *looks at her.*

Nanna   Bring him back and I swear I'll never, never speak like that to him again . . .

Shadow   But obviously you will. And if I can see that, then presumably so can the Lord. He knows you're lying to him.

Nanna   I mean it, Lord. Never a harsh word from me again.

Nanna *waits for an answer.*

Shadow   Fine.
Fine, if that's the way you want it.

Shadow *steps towards her.*
He reaches out, and touches his finger just above her left breast.
Nanna *gasps in pain and falls to the bed.*
Shadow *stands over her.*

Shadow   Don't you fucking cry now, you asked for that.

Katie   You won't leave me.

Beat.

You won't leave me burned and crying and on my own.

Luke   I think I heard my nanna.

Katie   Luke!

Shadow   No!

Katie   You promised.

Luke *runs.*
He goes to **Nanna***, lying on his bed.*
Shadow *watches.*

Luke   Nanna?
(*Beat.*) Nanna, are you all right?

Nanna   I came in and your bed was empty, and I was
worried sick /

Luke   I'm sorry, I couldn't sleep, I went for a walk.

Nanna   Thank God you're all right.
(*She hugs him again.*) I don't know what I'd do /

Luke   The woods and the river looked so pretty, I wanted
to have a wander round. See it all properly.

Nanna   I thought –
– I don't know what I thought.

Shadow *turns away; goes over to* **Katie***.*

Shadow   Listen: you just sit tight there, and I'll fetch him
back now.

Nanna   Lay down now, and I'll tuck you in.

Luke *gets into bed and lies down.*

Nanna   Promise me you'll stay away from that Katie.

Luke   Nanna –

Nanna   It's not that she's – she's not a bad girl, it's just . . .
There's things you're too young for.

Luke   I promise, Nanna.

Beat.

Nanna   All right, then.
Goodnight.

Luke   Night-night, Nanna.

Nanna *goes to leave. She pauses.*

Nanna   You don't want . . . you don't want Nanna to sleep in with you tonight, do you, if you're having trouble dropping off?

Luke   I'll be fine, Nanna.

Nanna   'Course you will.

She leaves. **Shadow** *comes over.*

Shadow   She's crying.

Luke   I can't.

Shadow   Really badly.

Luke   I promised Nanna.

Shadow   You promised Katie first.

Luke *doesn't answer.*

Shadow   She needs you.

Luke   I can't.

Shadow   And you need her more.

Beat.

Luke   I promised my nanna.

They look at each other.

Shadow   This is not how it's supposed to be.

Luke   I know.

Beat.

Shadow   Fine. If that's the way you want / it.

Luke   / It's not.
It's not the way I want it at all.

Shadow *turns and walks back to* **Katie**.

Shadow *stands over* **Katie**.
Eventually **Katie** *looks up at him.*

Shadow   Look. I'm sorry.
This has
Really not gone according to plan.
But – they're not going to beam me back
Till they get the signal for mission complete, so
I'm fucked too, you know.

Katie   So will you stay?

Shadow   Me? I can't *stay*.
No, that's not my mission, you don't –

Katie   If I'm burned, will you hold me?

Shadow (*beat*)   You don't get it at all.

Katie   Will you find the bits of me that aren't burned, and
hold me?

Shadow   No, that's not my mission.
I'm not equipped for any of that. (*He looks to* **Luke**.)

Luke   They're called forensic scientists.
The people who find out what happened
In crashes and murders and things.
They talked to my Nanna.
Smiling when they looked down at me.
But very very serious when they talked to Nanna.
(*Beat.*) I was tiny then, clinging on to Nanna's legs.
They must have thought I . . . couldn't hear.
They must've thought I couldn't put the words together.
(*Beat.*) They told Nanna that the way the car crashed had
trapped my mum inside.
The steering wheel was crushed into her chest, and her legs
were gone through the dash.
But my dad, he could get out.
He crawled out of the window and got free.
(*Beat.*) And then he crawled back in.
He got back in so he was killed when it all exploded.

And he never came to check on me.

(*Beat.*) He wanted to come and check on me, I know.
But with all them bits of car in her and broken glass
everywhere, and petrol, and her in pain and knowing she
was gonna die – he couldn't let my mummy go through that
alone.

And so he had to leave me alone.

(*Beat.*) That wasn't how things were supposed to be, I know.
But that was the best. That was the best he could manage.

Shadow   That's not my mission.
I'm not equipped.

Katie *moves closer to* **Shadow**.
Shadow *doesn't move away*.
Katie *reaches out to hold him*.

Shadow   I'm not – for this.

Katie *stops*.

I'm just a trick of the light.

Katie *looks at him*.
She takes his hand.

The Drowned World

My thanks to all at Paines Plough, to the Pearson Playwrights'
Scheme for giving me the time to think my way into this one
and to Michael McCoy.
Diolch o galon i ti, Catrin.

for Vicky Featherstone

The Drowned World was first performed at the Traverse Theatre, Edinburgh, on 1 August 2002. The cast was as follows:

Darren   Neil McKinven
Tara   Josephine Butler
Kelly   Eileen Walsh
Julian   Theo Fraser Steele

Directed by Vicky Featherstone
Designed by Neil Warmington
Lighting by Natasha Chivers
Music and Sound by Nick Powell

Scene One

Julian *and* **Tara** *carry themselves as if they are radiantly beautiful.* **Darren** *and* **Kelly** *do not.*

Darren   I get to the station with still some hope left.
I climb to the platform, and I have still some hope left: hope for a moment of lightheadedness, a surface slippery and wet, a loss of balance, an unexpected meeting of mind and escalator.
No such luck.
I make it to the train intact.
I find a seat. I sit down.
The faces around me stretch and settle into a protective blankness and –
Ahead of me, a foot stretches out.
It stretches from the toe, lifting off the ground into the air, pointing, pulling the rest of the leg into line behind it. The skirt draped around the leg falls away, it falls away along the line of a split that goes right up to the thigh, and I see toe and foot and calf and thigh stretched out, and even though I can't see . . . face, from watching the muscle define itself in the underside of her calf it's as if I'm looking into her eyes, drinking in her lazy, luxuriant pleasure in the sensation of the tendons tightening all along her leg.
Her hand reaches down, and pulls the skirt back over the thigh as the leg relaxes and lowers itself back to the floor.
At the next stop I stand, turn away from her, walk through the carriage and get off the train at the far end. I walk along the platform to the doors just in front of her, and hop back on.
I sit down opposite her. I don't meet her eyes as I sit.
I can't.
I don't need to.
I watch her reflection reading a paperback as the train flashes past towns and villages and the people and the lives, the worlds within them –
– all these worlds glide under the surface of her skin, she contains whole worlds within her.

Whole worlds I could escape into.
I watch her reflection in the window and I know –
– she is the angel sent to save me.
The train draws into the East Central Station and I don't
move.
I don't join the crowds of busy citizens bustling to get off.
I don't join the crowds of suits and students bustling to get off.
I sit there and so does she. I wait for her to lean over and
gently touch me on the arm and say something simple and
beautiful, maybe just say hello and suggest we go for a coffee
or a drink.
We'll sit down. She'll have a mineral water and smile
indulgently as I order a crisp German beer. I'll explain that
in her absence it has become my habit to take a reviving
draught of lager at around ten each morning. She'll let me
get away with it but her smile will be saying – six months
and I promise, you won't be needing that rubbish in your
system . . .
I sit and wait for her to make her move and she puts away
her book and looks up and I look up and finally our eyes
meet and she –
– this angel smiles at me –
– and she stands and goes to the door and gets off the train.
She walks along the platform, down the stairs and away into
the crowd.

Beat.

I see her again as I'm walking to work, of course.
I see her in a blonde waving high denomination notes at a
cabman outside the station.
I see her in a brunette sat on a number 18 bus pulling into
Wood Street.
I see her in this thin, elf-faced girl sitting drinking coffee at
the Hayes Island Refreshment Bar who looks for all the
world like a perfectly lit kinograph star –
I see her again and again and each time as I pass I focus my
mind and send a telepathic burst saying – here I am, here
I am, I'm the one you've been sent to save so now *turn
around* –

– and say hello or touch my arm or smile and we can just take it from there, please. Please.

Just one moment of warmth, please. Just one graspable moment. One instant of care I can refer back to in times of unease or discomfort. Something to be an anchor. To keep me from drifting off. To keep me from sliding under. To – Obviously I'm not saying I'm anything special – I'm of course entirely ordinary but ordinary people don't have to struggle on month after month after month without a kiss or a cuddle or a smile smiled for them and them only –

Beat.

– I'm being brushed past, I'm receiving glancing blows –
– to my elbows and my back –
– and I can't bear even the least impression of these people –

Beat.

I realise my mistake.
The angel is coming *for me.*
I don't have to go looking for her.
She's going to come for me.

Beat.

That was the last time I set foot outside.

Tara   I tread water, just below the surface of sleep.
I float there for as long as I can.
I'm like a body trapped in the ribs of a shipwreck.
When I wake the seabed shifts, the body is set free and the gases of decay send it shooting through the surface.

Kelly   I'm up today hours before I need to be.
I doze off easily enough, but sleep can't keep a hold on me.
At dawn I give up.
I go down to the harbour. I sit on the quay and watch the grey waves, rolling off the horizon, battering themselves against the sea walls.

Tara   When I wake, when I fall up through the surface of sleep, his arms are there to catch me.

His arms mark out the limits of the world: the world's
breath warms the back of my neck; its fingers gently stroke
my hair; the world loves me.
These are the moments I will try to remember when I find
myself . . . polishing a window or pruning a rose bush in the
garden and without warning I appreciate the sheer
ridiculousness of carrying on and I'm tempted to take the
shears, and hack into the plant, to hack it ragged, to sink the
shears in and watch its sap ooze out, watch its heartwood
dry out and die in the sun.
I'll resist that temptation. I'll remember those first few
moments of the day, when the world loved me. And I'll
prune the rose bush. I'll pick moss out of the lawn. I'll weed
the herb garden, and breathe in the mint and the rosemary.
I'll do these things aware that tomorrow the whole place
might be doused in petrol.
Because they would.
They will.
They'll burn the garden. They'll see we care about it and so
they'll burn it.
Once they've finished with the house.
Before they start on us.

Kelly   Walking back into the heart of the city, I see a kid.
Eight, nine years old, on this ragged old horse, riding
bareback, clinging on to its mane.
There's a smile in his eyes.
A shout of pleasure forming in his mouth.
No citizen would dare be out of doors, breaking curfew.
No citizen would ride like he owns the street. Like the city is
his.

Beat.

I reach inside my jacket. I click open my holster.

Tara   I couldn't wake alone.
I couldn't do for him what he does for me.
I can't imagine how anyone could.
I wonder what must be in his heart, that he can take all this
and still have strength left to comfort me.

Kelly   The leather of the holster gives the slightest creak, surely too soft a sound to carry – but as my hand curls around the grip of my pistol, he becomes aware of me.
He becomes aware he's being looked at.
The smile dies on his face. And his eyes are sunken, his mouth twisted and sulky, muscles under his cheeks withered.
My gaze slides off him.
He's one of us. He's a citizen.
I wave, so he'll see my hand is empty, and understand he's in no danger.
I wave, but I can't bear to look at . . . that mouth, those eyes.
The pony's hooves crack on the cobblestones as the boy gallops away.

Tara   We lie in bed, holding each other, and Julian tells me stories about what we're going to do with the day.
We'll get up, wash, get dressed; we'll make breakfast and then do the breakfast dishes, and so on and so forth; we talk the day out, we talk through every detail so we can see it stretching ahead of us.
You see, he tells me, they can't come today. Because –
There are so many things that need doing today – we simply haven't got *time* for them to come.
And so we get up: like citizens.
We get on with the day, like citizens.

Kelly   I pick up my squad from the barracks. One with oozing skin, one with ruined teeth.
I lead them through the city. They're excited: chattering like schoolchildren behind my back.
They've never carried out a quarantine order before.

Tara   They won't come for us today, like they didn't come for us yesterday.

Kelly   We stand for a moment outside the house.
It seems deserted.
But perhaps they're just asleep.
I wonder if they do sleep.
Or if they just go to bed, and lie there, waiting.

Tara   Except.
I've taken the loaf from the bread bin. I've put it down on
the table. I've gone to the drawer and I'm pulling the bread
knife from the drawer and –

Kelly   Knock knock.

Tara (*to* **Julian**)   Who's that?

Kelly   Knock knock.

Tara *looks at* **Kelly**.

Julian   Don't worry: I promise you.
It's not them.
They haven't come for us.
It's just –

Kelly   Just kids.

Julian   It'll just be kids. Trying to panic us.
So don't give in to them.
Don't give them what they want.

Kelly   They're just kids.
Neither of them a day over eighteen.
Ruined teeth and oozing skin.
Waiting for me to give the order.

Julian   The idea was to go with some dignity.
To keep some dignity about us, for as long as that was
possible.
When they came we would just –
– we wouldn't resist.
We wouldn't make a fuss or try to escape.
We wouldn't offer them any kind of distraction.
We would let them focus on what they had come to do.
And we hoped /
/ I hoped, if they saw clearly what they were doing –

Kelly   Oozing skin and ruined teeth, they can't wait to get
down to business.

Julian   What I did wrong was –

I went to the window.
Just in case. Just to check.

Beat.

It wasn't seeing the soldiers that made me doubt.
It wasn't the hooks, or the gloves, or the rope. It wasn't the little tub of paraffin or the tindersticks, for setting light to our bodies afterwards.
It was the officer. It was the sheet of paper in her hand. The quarantine order.
No matter how little noise we made. No matter how much time and space we gave them to think, there would be the quarantine order telling them: ignore any queasiness or shortness of breath. These reactions can be distressing, but are entirely normal. Carry on with your duty, and these physical pangs will soon correct themselves.

Beat.

They're not a confident people.
I hoped they might have been persuaded.
On an individual level.
I was sure they could be.
But they came with a piece of paper. An order. Giving clear instructions on how to deal with the bodies.
I hadn't thought of that.

Tara   I remember the moment.
He went to the window, pulled back the drape and
He didn't move, he didn't jump
But he seemed to flicker.
He seemed to not quite be there.

Kelly   Later, the inquisitor asked me about the initial moment of exposure.
I told him: the house was dark, the curtains drawn. I remember looking at my reflection in the window, and the curtains parted, and there was a man's face on the other side of the glass.
The inquisitor asked, what physical sensations were

experienced at this time? I said: I felt sick. I felt like the
insides of my stomach had gone missing.
The inquisitor nodded and said, this indicates the radiance
penetrated to your internal organs. What happened next?
I told him – I looked directly into the man's eyes. In his
eyes, there was my reflection, and it was tiny and twisted.
What sensations were experienced at this point, the
inquisitor asked.
I told him: I felt tiny and twisted.
The inquisitor nodded.
What happened next, he asked.
And then I fell on to the pavement, and I found I was crying.
The inquisitor nodded again. Yes, he said. Loss of moral
control. That is the next stage of the radiance sickness.

Tara   In my hand is the bread knife.
I've run out of the house, down the alley and through the
streets and I'm still carrying this bread knife.

Beat.

I stop running.
It takes Julian a few seconds to sense I've fallen behind.
He turns, slowing but not quite coming to a halt.
Their footsteps are close, and he doesn't dare shout at me to
come on, to catch up with him.
He stares, and his stare pleads.

Kelly   The inquisitor puts his arm round me.
I pull back, but he holds me there.
He says – you understand now, don't you.
You understand how dangerous they are.
You understand now why all sources of radiance have to be
removed.
He holds my gaze. I nod.
He smiles at me.
I hand over my pistol.

Tara   Julian.
Sometimes, when we're together.
We're together in bed.

I cry out or clutch you the wrong way and you stop, you
pull back, you wipe the sweat from my forehead and you
search my face and I can see you thinking – have I hurt her?
Have I?
Think about that.
Think how careful you are with me.
When they catch us, it'll be the exact opposite.
Not your gentle fingers teasing me open, but their ragged
nails forcing a way in. Not your kisses, but their curses and
spit.

Julian   They might not catch us.

Tara   Not your face, but a half-dozen of theirs, peering
down their snouts at me, wondering 'Have we hurt her?
Have we hurt her yet?'

Julian   I won't let them / [touch you]

Tara   / Two of them hold you, while the other ten beat
you senseless. Once you're broken on the floor, they'll turn
their attention to me. They'll prop bits of you up so you can
admire their technique.
But. Now there's just us. And –
– I've got this knife.

Julian *looks.*

Kelly   I'm shaking again.
What is it, the inquisitor asks. You may as well just say.
I tell him –
– those eyes.
I want them.
I want them to be mine.

Tara   We've got this moment.
We have this opportunity
to put ourselves out of harm's way.
Now: quickly.
Before they find us, and make us less than we are.

Julian   Even as she placed the knife – I was proud.

Tara   I put my arm, my left arm, round his neck.
I pull him close.
The point slides in an inch and then bounces back like a
spade hitting rock –
– he staggers, falls forward, falls to his knees and I hold him
up and now I can lean in, use my weight to drive the point
deeper, and as the knife's teeth scrape against bone, I pull
him tight, I catch his eyes –

Julian   Her face – the blade got stuck and something
came in to her eyes –

Darren   I've not left the house since. I've not.
I've sat, and I've waited for the knock on the door.
And –
– it's not a knock, it's . . . a thump.
I count to five and I – look through the peephole and –
she's staring right at me.
I throw back the bolts and the chains and I open the door –
– he stumbles on to me.
I catch him –
– there's this handle sticking out of him, and I grab it and
pull and it's a knife, it was so far in him I couldn't even see
the blade, and now there's all this blood –
– he's too heavy so I let him slide down to the floor –
– she's standing at the doorway, looking at me.

Kelly   His eyes.
I want them.
I want them to be mine.

Darren   There are sirens and boots crunching along the
street.
I've got no voice.
I don't need a voice.
Because: she knows.
She steps over the threshold.
She turns the locks and slides the bolts.
She's come.

Kelly   I want those eyes to be mine, I tell him.

You can have them, he says.
You can have them for your very own.
You just have to find them.

Scene Two

Darren   When I still went to work.
When I could still bear to leave the house and go to work,
my last project at the ministry involved cataloguing certain
sound recordings.
The recordings were made by putting a subject into a
carefully miked room, and tying the subject to a chair. And
then forcing a hose down the subject's throat. And then
putting a funnel in the top of the hose. And then pouring
bleach into the funnel.
The recordings were created for morale purposes: they
would be broadcast over the far-speaker network to stiffen
the resolve of the citizenry, in the event of a collapse of
national moral will.
The subjects involved in these recordings were citizens who
had tried to help non-citizens evade quarantine orders.

Beat.

I have listened to these recordings at length, over the course
of the project. And yet I wasn't worried when the police
came round conducting routine door-to-door. I wasn't
worried about their counters clicking away, measuring
ambient radiance. I wasn't worried about the bloodstains on
the floor. Because everything was going to plan, and the
plan did not include the police dragging me off to the dark
rooms under the ministry.
If anything, it was the bloke that was worrying me. 'Cause I
didn't know what he was *for.*
But he didn't worry me too much: because he was obviously
going to die.

Tara   When the police came we hid in the cellar. Julian
was still drifting in and out of consciousness and I –

I didn't think this guy was going to say anything. I can
imagine life takes a sudden, dark turn for citizens who get
caught sheltering our sort.
It was just: what if they come in. What if they search the
place. What if they see all the blood on the hall floor –
And Julian was still drifting.
I was on my own.

Darren   After the police went, I left a discreet pause. I
didn't want to bother her immediately.
Not after what had clearly been a stressful morning.
(*To* **Tara**.) What do you want to do?
I'd suggest we go to a café, but that's not really on
what with the curfew, and the cops looking for you, and
everything.
But we could have a drink here.

Tara   I'm sorry?

Darren (*beat*)   I've got tea.
I've got water, not sparkling but bottled at least.
You can't trust the taps these days, can you.

Waits for a response from **Tara***: none comes.*

Perhaps you're in the mood for something stronger.
It's my habit to take a reviving draught of German lager at
about this time of day.
Obviously I can't get German lager.
I have, however, extensive supplies of clear spirit they sell in
five-litre plastic flagons. I bought it in bulk, before they
brought in the rationing. I had a little warning, you see:
contacts at the ministry.

Waits for a response from **Tara***: none comes.*

I expect you're going to tell me I shouldn't be touching that
rubbish.
Aren't you.
You're going to tell me I don't need that crap in my system.
Well.
I'm sure you'll wean me off it soon enough.

Tara   What the hell are you talking about?

Darren   Just saying now you're around I won't be
needing to hit the bottle quite so much, will I.
I say bottle, I mean, of course, five-litre plastic flagon.

Tara (*stares at him*)   Jesus Christ.

Beat.

Darren   So . . . do you want some tea?

Tara   No, thank you.

Darren   Or some –
– or some stovecakes?
I've got some stovecakes left, I could heat them up for you /

Tara   / Will you just – leave me alone? Please?

Beat.

Darren (*to* **Tara**)   You could be a bit more –

Tara's *look cuts him off.*

Darren   You don't have to take it out on me.
It's not my fault, all this.
I've just tried to *help*.

Beat.

Tara   I've heard.
I've heard these rumours about factories.
Rendering factories where they send the corpses of diseased
animals and rip out their spines and brains and hearts, so
the disease can be contained.
The rumours say – our kind end up in these factories.
What the rumours don't say.
What I don't understand is –
– which part of us do you think is diseased? Our brains?
Our hearts? Our nerves, what?

Darren   None of those.

Kelly   None of that.

Tara   What is it about me that's diseased?

Darren   These factories –

Kelly   It's your skin.

Darren   – I used to work at the ministry.

Kelly   Your smile.

Darren   I worked keeping records.

Kelly   Your *eyes*.

Darren   These factories – (*Dries up.*)
Referendum day.
I wanted to vote and say they should leave you alone.
But I couldn't –
– find a way to leave the house.
Because out on the streets.

Beat.

It was bad enough when they let your lot walk around the
place. Mid-conversation one of you'd swan past and –
– everything stopped for a few seconds.
We'd pull ourselves together and struggle to pick back up
whatever we were talking about before the sparkle in your
eyes or bounce in your hair made whatever we were talking
about seem small, ridiculous, laughable . . .
Then when they got you off the streets . . .
Without you there was just us.

Beat.

Our –

Kelly   – oozing skin. Our ruined teeth.

Darren   Talking about whatever small, ridiculous,
laughable things we had to talk about. With no hope that
one of you might walk past and /
/ I couldn't bear it.
Those *faces*.

Beat.

She can't even look at me.
She can't meet my eyes.
Her gaze slides right off me.
How can she save me if she can't even look at me?

Kelly   She can't save you, obviously.

Tara   We'd never do this to you.
We'd try to help, if there was a problem.
We'd never exterminate your kind, just to save ourselves.
We'd rather die.

Beat.

Darren   How is he?
Your friend.

Tara (*looks at* **Darren**) He's fine.

Turns away from him.

He's fine except he can't speak.

His eyes flick open occasionally but they don't focus
properly: they focus on empty points in the room. Like he's
seeing into another world. Like he's leaving me already.

Beat.

And I don't know what to do.
We had plans.
He told me a story about the day that involved cutting back
the rhododendrons and pruning the roses. It didn't involve –
Any of this.
And he's asleep.
He's left me alone.
I hug him and his breath
Sets the hairs of my neck on end
He's wrapped in blankets
Blankets this citizen gave us
He smells of them
He smells like a citizen

I pull them off and bury my head in his chest
I open his shirt so I can taste his skin: and it tastes of blood
I open my eyes and I can see into the cut
I can see
I can see his heart.
The cold of the basement
is freezing it.
I can see ice crystals
Forming inside the cut.
He is freezing from the inside out.

Darren   It's this bloke.
It's 'cause this bloke's still here.
That's what's fucking things up.

Tara   He agreed with me it was best that we just –
– take care of ourselves before they could get to us.

Darren   He's supposed to get her here, to me, and then –
– he dies, right?
I sit with him. I watch him breathing.
Really shallow breathing.
He could go any moment, the blood he's lost.
I could wait for that moment.
Or I could pick up a pillow.

Tara   He'd given his consent.

Darren   Push it over his face.

Tara   And they did come, the police did come for us.

Darren   He's barely conscious anyway.

Tara   He'd promised they wouldn't, but they did.

Darren   Or if he is conscious, he must be in dreadful pain.

Tara   He agreed it was for the best.

Julian *looks at her.*

Tara (*meets his gaze; looks away; to* **Darren**)   You know what
you can do.

If you want to do something for us.

Darren   What? What d'you need?

Tara   We can't get away.
He's too –
– Julian's too weak to move.

Darren   I know; perhaps some sweet tea, or I have a little broth /

Tara   / I don't think broth is going to be enough to make him better. I think he's going to die.

Darren (*beat*)   I think you're very brave to face up to that.

Tara   Rather than waiting and running the risk that the police will find us and do God knows what I'm going to end it.
And when I've done that.
If you want to make up.
If you want to make up for all the things your people have done to us.
I've got this knife.
I want to go with him.
I won't know what to do unless he's there to –
I don't want to wake up and know the world hates me.

Beat.

If I can't finish the job.
Will you do it for me?

Darren *looks.*

Tara   If you don't want to use the knife, you could use a pillow or something, you could just put it over my head. Please.

Darren   I can't.

Tara   You really have to.

Julian   I wake up and the first thought that forms in my

mind is: did Tara have time to kill herself before they got to
her?
I imagine it is this thought that makes me sorry.

Tara   Honey.

Julian   I woke up and I was alone.

Tara   I was here, sweetheart. I haven't left you.

Julian   But I woke up and it was dark and I was alone.

Tara   You must've –
– that must've been a dream, sweetheart. If you wake up
and I'm not here – that's just a dream. I'd never leave you
alone.

Julian   I remember: turning away from her.
The strength draining from my legs.
Falling into a door: and then the door collapsing under my
weight.
Not collapsing. Opening. The door opened.
This – citizen – let us in.

Tara   Yes he did.

Julian   I look at him. He has –
– the look of all good citizens: damp, waxy skin, a bed for
mosses and fungus. Fingers as rough and stubby as twigs.
And eyes –
(*To* **Darren**.) What's your name?

Darren   I'm called Darren.

Julian   In his eyes –
(*To* **Darren**.) – why did you help us?

Darren (*looks*)   I even want to tell him.
I want to be honest with him now, in his last moments.
I want to thank him for bringing her to me.
I want to tell him: I let you in because I had no choice. I was
going to die if she hadn't come to save me. And I really
don't want to die.

Julian   He stutters and flails for words.
(*To* **Darren**.) It's OK. I understand. You let us in because
you had to.

Darren *looks at him.*

Julian   You had to because you don't want to die.

Darren *nods.*

Julian   Soon enough, they'll have killed every last one of
us.
Processed the bodies. Buried the evidence at sea.
Then the ministry will start work on your people. They'll get
rid of anyone who carries an echo of our kind.
Each one of you who is touched by the ghost of us – filtered
out.
And that's how you'll die.
The ministry will blame it on agents introduced into the
water supply by hostile Western powers.
Or sunspot activity.
Or an unfavourable alignment of the planets.
But you'll know the truth.
Won't you.

Darren *looks at him.*

Julian   You won't be able to stand the sight of each other.
First, it'll be babies abandoned on the streets because
mothers can't bear to look at them.
Then no babies at all, because you can't bear to come near
one another.
And then those of you who are left will wither and die
For the want of one moment of warmth.
For the want of a smile.

Beat.

You can feel it coming, can't you?
You can feel all that coming for you.
(*To* **Tara**.) I was an idiot.
I should have known it would be an ordinary citizen.

An ordinary citizen who looked out of his window, and saw
us and simply couldn't let us die.
Because he understood we're all the same.

Darren   But – we're not.
I'm not the same as you.

Julian   If they find us here, what will happen to you?

Kelly   A visit to a carefully miked-up room.
A funnel, a hose shoved down the throat.

Julian   You sheltered us to save yourself; I know that. But
it doesn't matter.
You sheltered us: you put yourself in our shoes.

Darren   She can't meet my eyes.
Her gaze slides right off me.
Because I'm.
Because I am the way I am, and no more.

Julian   When you sheltered us, you joined us.
You made yourself the same as us.

Darren   No, you don't –
I don't think you understand.

Julian   I do understand.
Whyever you think you sheltered us.
Whatever you think the reason was.
It doesn't matter.

Darren (*beat*)   He tries to reach up to me from the bed.
The rags bandaging his chest are brown with stale blood.
From the wound itself, a sweet sharp smell.
It's a smell –
– that reminds me of walking in a forest.
Dappled green light. Seven years old. With a girl – her
name was –
– not important.
Pushing through brambles, we came to a clearing and
suddenly the air was heavy and sweet.
She bent down, as if she was going to pick a flower.

And held up the skull by one of its horns. She held it up for me to see – and the whole thing came apart.
The horn came apart from the skull, and the skull fell to the floor and cracked open, and the brain popped out: except it wasn't the brain, it was a ball of maggots and flies that dissolved into the air around us.
We both ran out of the forest and into the fields and she cried and cried and I thought she'd never stop.

Beat: he looks to **Tara**.

And that was my first ever kiss.

Beat.

He hugs me, and reaches out to the woman, and pulls her close, pulls her arms around him, and so pulls her arms around me.
I can feel the warmth of her against my back.

Beat.

(*To* **Julian**.) We're going to need food, then.
If you're going to stay.

Julian   Of course we're going to stay. Because this is how it begins. This is how the change comes. From the three of us.

Darren   My rations won't be enough.
But there are people you can go to, if you've got stuff to sell.

Tara   Have you got anything we can sell?

Darren   No.
But you have.

Scene Three

Kelly   The inquisitor said:
We are close to a generalised solution to the problem of the
non-citizenry. At this time, however, ground actions are still
useful.
It is in this aspect that we propose to deploy you.
I had been instructed to remove my uniform.
I stood, naked.
The inquisitor looked away. Obviously.
An under-secretary arrived with civilian clothes. Averting
his eyes, he placed them on the floor next to me.
You will dress, and go out into the city.
What will I do to be of service to the ministry, I asked.
There are collaborators, the inquisitor told me, who shelter
non-citizens. Inevitably, they become infected with traces of
radiance. The very susceptibility that left you unable to
carry out this quarantine order makes you useful in tracking
these collaborators.
Your moral weakness, your vulnerability to infection, your
sensitivity to radiance, will lead you to them.

Beat.

They let me go.

Darren *seems to hear her.*

Kelly   They set me loose.

Darren *is aware of her voice.*

Kelly   I found myself down by the harbour.
I found him.

Beat.

He . . . presented himself to me.

Darren *looks at her.*

Kelly (*looks back at him*)   He made a gift of himself to me.
(*To* **Darren**.) Hello.

Darren   Hi. (*He looks away.*)

Kelly   I imagined I would feel some – trepidation.
But then I looked at him.
At his –
– skin hair throat *eyes* –
– and it was fine.
I wanted him –
– taken away.
Removed from my sight.
I mean –
– something – a sulk, carved into his cheek,
Something that brought down the tone of the planet,
Something that made it so much easier.
Something –

Beat.

That reminded me of myself.
(*She looks at* **Darren**.) Hello

Darren   Hi.

Kelly   You fucking – filthy fucking –
– are you really going to make this
So fucking easy for me you fucking –
(*She catches herself; smiles at* **Darren**.)
I give the nod to the plainclothes butchers
Who've been assigned to me.
(*Looks at him.*)
Have you got . . .

Darren *looks at her.*

Kelly (*holds his gaze, then:*)   Have you got something . . . to
sell?

Darren *looks away.*

Kelly   Because I'm looking to buy.
If you've got anything.
Whatever you might have, I'm in that market.

Darren   I've got some . . . stuff.

Kelly   Hand it over, then.

Beat.

Don't get all tense.
Don't look at me.
Don't pretend not to be doing anything.
Just sit there, look at the sea, look at the sea gulls, and then
when you're ready, without warning, without any great big
fuss, take the package from under your jacket and give it to
me. (*Looks at him.*)

Darren *looks at her.*

Kelly   What?

Darren   Don't you want to –
– check out . . . the merchandise?

Kelly *looks at him.*

Darren   I'm sorry if that's really naïve.
I've never done this before –

Kelly   – yes I do.
Yes of course I want to.

Beat.

Go ahead then.

Darren   Out here?
In the open?
You want me to –
– show you the stuff?
In the open? Where people will see?

Kelly   The butchers are closing in.
Reaching under their regulation trenchcoats
For their regulation skin-shavers
Their regulation finger-snippers
Their regulation eye-hooks.
(*Beat. To* **Darren**.) We'll go –

We'll get some privacy.
I give another nod to the butchers.
This nod says: just, back off.
Just, keep your distance.
Don't scare the little baby away.

Darren   She leads me up an alley.

Kelly   Let's have a look then.

Darren *looks at her.*

Kelly   He was nervous –
– but there was something else as well.

Beat.

I went to take the package from him and his grip tightened
round it.
He didn't want to let it go.

Darren   You –
– don't look with your hands.

Kelly (*looks at him; smiles*)   No you don't.
And he reached in to the package.
And pulled out –

Beat.

– oh my God . . .

Darren   I watched Julian gather her hair in his hand, like
he was going to make a ponytail.
I said, when he went to sharpen the blade, I told him he was
getting it wrong.
He said –

Julian   I know what I'm doing, trust me.

Darren   But I really think, the way you're doing it, I think
that makes the blade even duller –

Julian   – I think what's important is that we get this over
with as quickly as possible. I think what's important is that

we minimise the trauma of the experience for Tara.

Darren (*goes to reply to him; chickens out*)   The edge was still
dull when he started to cut.
He had to drag the knife through her hair like it was straw.
He hurt her.
It's not straw.
It's fine and soft and –

Kelly   – it picks up the sun, it spins and the sun sparkles
off it –

Darren   – and he hurt her.

Kelly   Bursts of silver light up the alleyway
Drain pipes and dustbin lids gleam and –
– oh . . .

Darren (*to* **Kelly**)   The money, please.

Kelly *looks at him.*

Darren   Can I have the money, please.

Kelly   Let me see it again.

Darren   You can.
You see it.
And – touch it.

Kelly *groans.*

Darren   And smell it.
And have it for your very own.
As soon as you hand over the money.

Beat.

Kelly   Where did you get that?

Darren *doesn't answer.*

Kelly   That looked . . . fresh.
She can't have been long dead
When you harvested that.

Darren   She wasn't –

Kelly   – wasn't . . . long dead.

Darren   No.

Kelly   Wasn't . . . dead at all?

Darren *can't answer.*

Kelly   He steps away from me.

Darren   If you don't want the stuff, that's just fine.

Kelly   Oh, I want it.

Darren   It's fine, I'll sell it somewhere else.

Kelly   And he –
– he's backing away and
He rubs his hand over his mouth
The hand that'd held her hair
And his mouth –

Darren   What?

Kelly   – his lips.

Darren   What are you –
– looking at?

Kelly   A sheen of light over his lips.

Darren   What are you – doing?

Kelly   A sheen of – radiance
Over his lips.
I step closer.

Darren   No.

Kelly   I close my eyes.

Darren   No.

Kelly   I have to because
His cheeks, his nose, his eyes
These are all unaffected.
But his lips.

Darren   Don't you –

Kelly   His lips.

Darren   Please.

Kelly   His mouth.

Darren   Oh God, no . . .

Kelly   The shine.
The radiance.

Darren   Don't – touch me . . .

Kelly   The radiance on his lips touches mine
– it's in me.

Darren   What have you done . . .

Kelly   I swallow it down.

Darren   What have you done to me?

Kelly   It's in me.
(*Beat; she smiles.*) The butchers . . .
Have been getting all worked up.
They've been stroking their blades under their trenchcoats.
The master butcher says:
Where'd he go? Where's the target?
I tell him: false alarm.
So fuck off.
Fuck off and let me do my job.

Beat.

And fuck . . . eyes
Fuck disappearing into some non-citizen's eyes.
I kissed one of my own kind, and
As our lips parted,
I managed to look at him
Even as our bodies touched.

Scene Four

Julian   You're back.

Darren   I am.

Julian *looks at him.*

Darren   What?

Julian   I don't know.
There's –
– did it go well?

Darren   I suppose.
How are you?

Julian   I'm... well. I suppose. (*Looks at him.*)

Beat.

Darren   What?

Julian   I don't know.
I think you've caught the sun.

Darren (*looks at him*)   I –
– haven't been out for a while.
So that could happen quite quickly, I suppose.

Julian   Looks good on you, a little bit of colour.

Darren (*looks at him, then:*)   Do you want to eat, then?

Kelly   When I get home, I go up into the loft.
Hidden away, under tea chests and mouldy clothes
I find a relic.
A framed advertisement for a Western cola drink.
This advertisement is printed on a mirror.

Julian   I'm starving.

Darren   And what about Tara?

Tara   I'm fine.

Beat.

Julian   She's fine, apparently.

Kelly   I prop the mirror on the mantelpiece.
I open the bag.
I pull out –
– I take it out.
I want to open the curtains so it will catch the light but
Of course I don't risk letting anyone see.

Julian   You should eat something.

Tara *doesn't answer.*

Julian   A few mouthfuls to keep your strength up.

Tara   As if you –

Julian   Please.

Beat.

Tara   Thank you.

Darren   You're . . . very welcome.

Kelly   I hold the hair up by my –
– I rub it over my face.
I breathe in its smell.
I tuck it behind my ears.
I lay it over my head.
I drape it in a fringe before my eyes.
I look in the mirror.
I look –
– ridiculous.
I look – (*She dries up.*)

Darren   This won't last forever, of course.

Julian   No.

Darren   We'll need more money.

Kelly   I look –

Beat.

I need more.

Beat.

Julian   Yes of course. (*He looks to* **Tara**.)

Tara *ignores him.*

Julian   Tara.

Beat.

Tara, will you fetch me the knife.

Beat.

Tara, will you fetch me the knife, please.

Darren (*quietly*)   No.

Julian   Tara will you fetch me the knife and the
whetstone. Please.

Darren   No.
No, you don't –
You're too weak.
You should rest.

Julian *looks at him.*

Darren (*beat; then:*)   As I draw the knife against the
whetstone, she shivers
I want to say: no. Don't –
– there's no need to be afraid.
I'm doing it right.
I'm making the blade sharper.
I'm making it easier.
I don't say that.
I just draw the blade against the stone.
I let her shiver.

Beat.

I gather her hair –
I touch her hair.
I touch her.

And she shivers.
I want to say, no, don't shiver,
I'm not –
– I'm doing this so we can be together –
– so we can live. So we can eat.

Beat.

Her hair is already cropped close by now
So I have to
Grip it quite tightly.
I have to
Bring the blade very close to her skin
And in doing this my knuckles brush against
Her scalp, the nape of her neck, her earlobes.

Beat.

And she shivers.
I want to say,
Please don't shiver at my touch.
Please don't –
– don't shiver like that.

Kelly   Hello again.

Darren *looks at her.*

Kelly   Didn't expect to see you back so soon.

Darren *says nothing.*

Kelly   I mean I hoped to.

Beat.

Darren   I've got more stuff.

Beat.

Kelly   OK.

Beat.

He lifts the bag towards me.
And his hands –

– his hands are gleaming.
I think those hands could touch me.
And neither of us would need to die.

Darren   Do you want it, then?

Beat.

Kelly   Yes. Please.

Darren   I'll need –
– the price has gone up, this time.

Kelly   That's fine.

Beat.

Darren   Good.

Kelly *looks at him.*

Darren   Well then.

Kelly   You're putting yourself in an awful lot of danger.

Darren *looks at her.*

Kelly   It's an awful lot of danger just – for money.

(*She looks at him.*)

It's not just for money, is it?
They're still alive.
You're sheltering them.
You're protecting them.

Darren *looks at her.*

Kelly   Why?

Darren   You wouldn't understand.

Beat.

Kelly   It's because you're going to die for want of a kiss
Or a smile
Or a touch

Beat. She reaches for him.

Darren   Don't.

Kelly (*pulls back*)   You could turn them in.
There are ways to turn them in
Without being . . . implicated.
I could help you. I have connections.

Darren   No.

Kelly   I kissed you.

Darren   No.

Kelly   And you didn't –

Darren   No.

Kelly   We could –

Darren (*looks at her*)   From her pocket, she pulls a lock of
Tara's hair
She rubs it over her mouth . . . and –

Kelly   You see?
Do you see?
Just – step closer.
Just close your eyes.
Just don't think of me.
I don't mind
If you think of her.
You have to think of her.
But it'll be me.
And we can be together.
We can use what we have of them
To be together
And make it bearable
And neither of us will need to die.

Beat.

There.
You see?

Darren *looks at her.*

Kelly   You see?

Darren *looks at her; turns away.*

Kelly   No. Don't . . .

Darren   / How do you know I can't have her?

Kelly   Oh God, don't . . .

Darren   / How do you know I can't have her properly?
How do you know she couldn't ever want me?

Kelly   Because . . .

Scene Five

Darren *looks at* **Julian**.

Julian   You were dreaming.

Darren   Yeah?

Julian   I was too.

Darren   You were too?

Julian (*nods*)   I think you were having a nice dream.
Weren't you?

Darren *doesn't answer.*

Julian   What were you dreaming of?

Darren   I – can't tell you.
What were you dreaming about?

Julian   Our glorious future. When we've triumphed over
the forces of darkness and returned the nation to sanity.
And we live together in peace. Brothers in the struggle . . .

Darren *laughs with him.*

Julian   Don't you fucking . . . giggle at my dreams.

Darren   I'm not laughing at your dreams, mate, just your –
I mean, 'brothers in the struggle'.

Julian (*smiles*)   Well: we are, aren't we?

Darren   Of course.

Beat.

Julian   But what?

Darren   Is Tara awake?

Julian *shakes his head.*

Darren   She –
She never looks at me.
She can never bring herself to look at me.

Beat.

Julian   Well, she –
She's afraid.

Darren   She's afraid of me?

Julian   It's not you: it's all the people you remind her of.
The soldiers. The ministry officials. The police.
Obviously you have the same . . . look.
It touches a nerve.

Darren   What kind of look?

Julian   I don't know, nothing in particular –

Darren   – tell me because if it's something I could change
I would if that would make things easier for Tara –

Julian   It's nothing, it's just –
I don't know.
It's nothing.

Beat.

It's nothing to do with you.
It's to do with other people.

We don't think about you –
– you're not like them.
You're like us.
You, me, Tara: we're the same.

Darren   I don't know if we are the same.
You know what to think, and what to do.
I get confused.
Sometimes I think – (*He looks at* **Julian**.)
– sometimes I see a cop in the street and I think I could just walk up to her and tell her all about you.
They'd come and take you away and I could throw myself on the mercy of the state. They'd probably kill me but –

Julian   You reckon I don't think about just running into the street? Letting them tear me to pieces?

Darren   I don't believe you.

Julian   Well: do. It's the truth.
The temptation to just end things
It's there all the time.
But I know I won't give in to it.
And I know you won't.

Darren *looks at him. Senses* **Tara** *– leaves.*

Tara (*watches* **Darren** *retreat*)   He's going to crack.

Julian   He is not.

Tara   Do you really get tempted?
To give in.
Do you?

Julian *looks at her.*

Tara   Of course you don't.

Julian   I told him what he needed to hear.

Tara   No, it's not that. I don't give a fuck what you tell him.
It's –

Julian *looks at her.*

Tara   We should try and get away.

Julian   I'm not well enough to travel.

Tara   You're not going to get any better here.

Beat.

He'd go with us. I bet he would.
He could be our cover. He could do the talking.

Julian   Do you really think so?

Tara   It's our best chance to get out of here alive.

Julian   Perhaps it is.

Tara   But you don't want to get out of here.

Julian   If they kill us all –

Tara   Serve them fucking right.

Julian   We're not worth more than the citizens.
Or do you disagree?
Do you think we are better than them?

Tara   No, obviously not.

Julian   They can all go to hell, so long as we two are
saved?

Tara   Why should it be me that has to stay here and at
any moment they could come through the door and take us
off and –

Beat.

If they come, it'll be me that has to live through it while they
do things to my body. It'll be me.

Julian   A nation can die, so long as we two are saved?

Tara   Yes: because –
– because they deserve to die.
Because they are killers.

And we are . . .

She dries up.

Julian   Pure?
Because we have never pulled triggers.

Tara   No.

Julian   We have never launched bombs.

Tara   No.
We would / never –

Julian   / We know nothing of the look that passes over a person's face when a blade touches them in places they've never been touched before.
No, you've never killed anybody.
You didn't quite manage it, did you.

Beat.

Tara   If we're staying, we'll need more money for food.

Julian   We will.

Tara   We'll have to find something else to sell.

Darren   I came awake from a dream where Tara was screaming –
– I sat shivering, waiting for my head to clear –
– and Tara screamed again.
(*To* **Julian**.) What's going on?

Julian *says nothing.*

Darren   What the fuck's going on?
Where's Tara?

Julian   She's in the bathroom.
She's fine.

Darren   What the fuck's been going on?

Beat.

His face is guiltless. Serene and unlined

as he open his hand –

Beat.

Seven years old.
This ram's skull exploding
And amidst the flies and shrapnel
Its teeth.
Much longer than you'd think.
They've got roots, sunk deep into the jaw.
So deep that if you try to pull them out you're almost bound
to crack the bone.

Beat.

– and he tips it out on to the table and raises the pliers –

Julian   I'll just smash the tooth so we can get to the
filling –

Darren   *No* –
– no, don't do that.
They – prefer it.
You get a higher price for the gold if the filling is still in the
tooth.
So they can be sure where it came from.
And what someone went through to give it up. (*He starts.*)

Tara   Sorry.

Beat.

Darren   Her mouth was like
When a child gets hold of lipstick and paints it round and
round out from her lips till her mouth takes over most of her
face.
She was pressing this rag to her jaw: when she took the rag
away blood bubbled up and filled her mouth.
On her jaw, I thought I could see –
There were what looked like.
He must have had to hold her jaw steady.
And there were these . . . indentations.
From where he must have put his boot.

Beat.

I saw all this.
I could see all that detail because
She looked at me.
She stared straight at me.
She let me look at her.
And she didn't mind.

Tara   Sorry about the noise.

Darren   And of course the surface matters
But that's OK.
That's OK now because
She has this ruined mouth
And now she will look at me
And although the surface affects the inside
If you were to hold your hand over that ruined mouth
You'd hardly be able to tell, from looking in her eyes
You'd hardly notice at all.

Tara   I'm sorry if we woke you up.

Darren   That's fine. It's no problem.
It's about time I was up anyway.
You know: taking actions. Doing things.
So that's really just fine.

Scene Six

Kelly   Hiya.

Darren   Hello.

Kelly (*beat*)   Were you looking for me?

He doesn't answer.

Have you got something to sell?

Darren   No.

Kelly (*looks at him*)   Yes you have.

Yes you have, I can / smell it

Darren   I don't want to deal with you any more.

Kelly (*beat*)   Perhaps you don't.
Tough bloody luck.
Let me see.

Kelly *looks at* **Tara**, *at the tooth.*

Oh my Christ.
It's . . . beautiful.
And there's still –
– there's still blood on it.
(*Looks at him.*) It's still alive.
We could knock one of my teeth out
And plant hers in the hole
Maybe it would take root in my jaw.
It would grow in me.
And then –
we could . . .

Darren *says nothing.*

Kelly   I know . . . you don't want to be alone.
You don't have to be.
If you could just . . .
. . . close your eyes and –

Darren   No.

Kelly *looks at him.*

Darren   No.

Kelly   You have to.

Darren   No.

Kelly   I'm your own kind.

Darren *looks at her.*

Kelly   We have to try.

Darren   I'd rather –

Beat.

How can we be together
When we know –

Kelly What?

Darren Look at me.
Go on. Look.
Look at it all.
Cast of skin and stink of mouth
And fear and shame and fear in the eyes.
How could you –
We could be together?
How could you be – with this?
When you know – *they exist.*

Kelly I could – close my eyes.
I could use my imagination.
I could – learn to bear it.
I could.
I think I really could.

Beat.

Do you think you could?

He doesn't answer.

Do you think you might?

He doesn't answer.

Do you –

Darren I think
I'd better deal with someone else from now on.

Kelly Darren.

Darren *looks at her.*

Kelly You're under arrest.

Darren *comes to a stop.*

Kelly   Don't look so shocked.
You knew who I was the second you set eyes on me.

Beat.

You knew I was coming for you.

Beat.

Who am I?

Darren   The police?

Kelly   I'm an angel.
I'm the angel come to save you.

Darren   I'm going to have to go now.

Kelly   You take one step and I'll shoot you . . .
. . . in the throat?
How'd you feel about that?

Darren   Not good.

Kelly   No.
Messy. Painful. Can take a while. Or it can be instant if the
bullet severs the spinal cord.
Now. Obviously I'm not a real angel, because real angels
don't go threatening to shoot people in the throat.
But I might be your angel.
Your guardian angel.

Beat.

I'm here to save your life.

Beat.

How this works is.
What you have to understand is –
– they're dead now.
These –

Darren   – people –

Kelly   – that you're sheltering.

They're dead.
Nothing you can do will change that.

She waits for a moment.

Now, given that they're dead, all that's left is you.
Your future.
And you might still have a future.
Traditionally, what you've done gets you a trip to a room
with an earth-packed floor.
The earth soaks up blood and other bodily fluids.
– The ministry need men like you. Men of your particular
. . . sensitivity.

Darren   You don't have to do this.

Kelly   I do, or I'll be killed.
The quarantine order has already been stamped and signed.
My controller keeps it in a briefcase which never leaves his
side.

Darren   You don't want to do this.
You –

Kelly   – what?

Darren   You like them.

Kelly   I like them?
Jesus Christ.
I like them?
If that was fucking all . . .
I would drown cities.
I would feed poison to children, then sit with them and
explain exactly how the toxin worked, even as it burned into
their organs.
I would paint your body with gentle acid that did not kill
you but let me peel your flesh away – the white, the pink,
the red – till only your bones remained.
All of this.
All of this and more.
To have one of them look at me

And not turn away
Not draw back
Not gag in disgust
For even a few seconds.

Beat.

And that is why we can't have these
Fatally radiant creatures
Walking round the place.
Reminding us how clumsy

Darren   and mean-spirited

Kelly   and graceless

Darren   and cowardly

Kelly   and shapeless

Darren   and flabby

Kelly   and foul we all are.

Beat.

Do you see?

Darren (*looks at her*)   I see.
But . . . if you met them –

Kelly *looks at him.*

Darren   – if you spoke to them –

Kelly   Don't.

Darren   – if you found out what they were like.

Kelly   We can't have them making us feel contempt for
our lovers
And shame for our children
And hate for our parents and . . . hate for our selves.

Beat.

But what we could do is.

Beat.

We. You and I.
We could have them.
Before we kill them.

Beat.

Darren   He wouldn't touch you.

Kelly   Not ordinarily.

But it's amazing what a man will bring himself to do if he believes his actions will preserve a woman's life.

Darren   And I don't want her. Not like that.

Kelly   You think you can't have her.
That's slightly different.
But you can.

Beat.

And you might as well, 'cause she's going to die anyway.
Or, I have you taken in.
I do what I want to the man.
I let a squad loose on the girl.
Who do you think will be gentler with her?

Darren *doesn't answer.*

Kelly   You can have her.
You can . . . find out what she is like.

Darren *looks away.*

Kelly   Will you take me to them?

Darren *doesn't answer.*

Kelly   Darren.

Beat.

Darren *looks up at her. Nods.*

Kelly *slowly smiles.*

Darren (*stares at her, then:*)   I led her down towards the harbour.
I didn't know quite how to go about it.
I put my arm round her.
Round the back of her neck.
I – played with her hair.
She shivered at my touch.

Kelly   Once they're gone, and you're safe
We can –
I don't want to kill them either
But given everything
Given that they're dead anyway.
Then once they're gone
We can be together
And – we can treasure them
We can share the memory of the time we had with them

Darren   I played with her hair, and she shivered.
Not in excitement. Obviously.
She shivered and then fought it down
I watched her fight it down, and smile,
Steel herself,
And lean in towards me,
And –

Kelly   They'll live on, in a way, through us.
That'll be nice, won't it: to keep them alive a little.

Darren   It will.

Kelly   We'll never have to be alone.
I can be with you, and you can be with me,
And when we're – together – it won't matter you're thinking about being with her
Because I'll be thinking about being with him.
You won't have to hate yourself for wanting one of them
'Cause I'll be wanting the exact same thing
But we'll never betray each other
We won't be able to
Because they'll all be dead and rotted and gone.

Darren   I watched her fight her shiver down,
Smile, and steel herself, and lean in towards me,
Her eyes closing, her lips just apart –

Kelly *cries out.*

Darren   I gripped her hair and pulled her back from me.
She started crying so I –
– I held her, by her hair, so she couldn't move or duck out
the way.
I hit her face.
She cried louder
So I kept hitting her
She quietened down and went all limp.
I let go her hair and – she just stood there,
She didn't try to run or nothing.
I didn't know what to do next.
There was this pole, like this iron pole with a hook that the
fishermen use for snagging the nets and lifting them out the
water.
She was just standing there, shivering.
I grabbed this pole and I hit her with it
I hit her in the face
And her jaw came apart
Teeth everywhere
Blood bubbling up from her mouth
She staggered back
And I hit her again
She staggered again, back towards the edge of the quay.
I kept hitting her
Knocking her back a few feet every time
Until she was right on the edge
I stuck the end of the pole in her belly
And just shoved.
She went flying off into the water.
It was like the water woke her up a bit
She started struggling and flapping around
Trying to stay afloat
Every time she went under I prayed that would be it
But she kept dragging herself back to the surface

So in the end I got the pole again and when she bobbed up
the next time
I threw it at her.
And that was it.

Beat.

I stood there at the side of the quay
Watching to make sure she didn't come up again.
Gradually the water calmed itself down.
I could see my reflection.
I could see myself.
I could see: a man staring into the water, praying and
praying that a girl was drowned.

Scene Seven

Tara   Hello.

Darren   Hi.

Tara   Are you . . . all right?

Darren   I've just been for a walk. Down by the quay.
Cleared a few things up.

Tara   OK.
I thought you were going to meet
the buyer.
And you were going to get us some food.

Darren   Yes I was.
But she didn't turn up.
She . . . I don't know.
I think the cops got her.

Tara   We're virtually out of water.

Darren   She'll be dead by now.

Tara (*looks at him*)   Her family can have my deepest
sympathies.

Darren   She's still –
I don't like it that people deal in your teeth and your hair
and –
Julian pulled it from your mouth but you've forgiven him
for that /

Tara   / He was just doing . . .

Darren   . . . what he had to do.

Beat.

How is he?

Tara   Worse.
I think he opened the wound again
When he –

Darren   – did what he had to do.

Beat.

I'll go and check on him /

Tara   / He's asleep, you should just leave him.

Darren   All right.

Beat.

Tara   I'm sorry about the girl. The buyer.

Beat.

Darren   She was fleecing me.
I'd've paid a million times what she did even to touch your
hair.

Tara *stares at him.*

Darren   Oh God, I didn't mean –
– that there's a price that would be enough.

Tara   Darren . . .

Darren   Because your hair should just stay on your
head.

Tara   Darren: it's OK. (*She smiles.*)

Darren (*smiles back*)   You shouldn't worry about Julian.

Tara   I know, he's going to be fine.

Darren (*beat*)   Yes he is.
He's got a constitution like a . . . horse. If that's what you say.

Tara   I think you can say that.

Darren   Then that's what he's got.

Tara   He's got faith, is what he's got.

Darren   And . . . you haven't.

Tara *shrugs. Beat.*

Darren   What?

Tara   I almost missed him.

Darren *looks at her.*

Tara   I wouldn't have seen myself with a guy like Julian.
In the long term.
Not before all this.

Darren   I can't –
I'm –
I'm very surprised to hear you say that.

Tara   Before things started to go to hell
I was
Apt to be distracted.
By pretty faces on the street.

Beat.

I could have just . . .

Darren   . . . passed him on the street.
Never looked twice.

Tara   I'd have looked twice.
He's quite striking.
I'd've looked. And I'd've touched. And I'd've taken.
But I might've just
Discarded him.
In the ordinary run of things
And never had a clue –
– what was in his heart.

Darren   There are blessings that come heavily disguised.

Tara   Yes there are.

(*She looks at* **Darren**.) What the fuck are you doing?

Darren (*looks at* **Tara**)   I was
Trying to comfort you /

Tara   / Get the fuck away from me.

Darren   I'm sorry.
I thought you –
I thought you were trying to tell me something.

Beat.

Tara   I was trying to tell you
How much I love –
How lucky I am to have found him.

Darren   Of course you were.

Tara   What did you / [think]

Darren (*turns to* **Julian**)   And how is Julian doing?

Julian   I'm –
I was dreaming.

Darren   Oh yeah?

Julian *nods.*

Darren   What were you dreaming of, Ju?

Julian   I dreamed – the sand on the beaches was ground

human bone.
And the mud at the bottom of the ocean was a compost of hearts and brains.
Someone tried to raise the dead and the mud found itself alive and it lived just long enough to scream before the ocean crushed it.

Darren   The usual, then.
And . . . what do you think that means, Julian?

Julian (*looks back at him*)   Do you think it means something?

Darren (*shrugs, then:*)   I'm fine, by the way. And thanks for asking.

Julian (*looks at him*)   Did you meet the buyer? Did you get food?

Darren   She didn't turn up.
Citizens: what can you do?
You certainly can't – depend on them.
You can't trust them.

Julian   Do you . . . know anyone else we can sell to?

Darren   They're fairly replaceable. I'm sure there'll be another one along soon.

Julian   Good, that's a / relief . . .

Darren   / So this dream: it's troubling you.

Julian (*beat*)   A little.

Darren   You don't know what it means.
Its meaning hasn't been revealed to you.
You find you're lacking an answer.

Julian   I suppose it seems . . . quite –

Darren   – apocalyptic?

Julian   Yeah.

Darren   Yes that's right. I'd've said that.
Though obviously I wouldn't until you had.

Julian (*looks at him*)   Darren.
What's going on?
What's up with you?

Darren *looks at him.*

Kelly   I'm lost.
I'm lost, and it's dark.
I'm sinking. I can tell that much.
I'm sinking, and I've already gone deeper than the sunlight
ever does.
There are monsters all around.
Some grey, and sleek, and full of teeth.
Some with tentacles and poison.
They're fighting.
They're fighting over me.
While the monsters fight there are smaller nightmares
Quivering jelly things attach themselves
To my face, my arms,
Semi-digesting me before they suck me in.

Darren   It's nothing.
I'm fine. I'm sorry.

Kelly   I've lost an arm. A grey thing swooped down and
tore it off.
The jelly creatures push their stomachs into the wound
Turning dark brown as my blood drains into them.

Darren   It's not nothing.
There's a problem.
Because the buyer didn't come, because she let me down.
I've got no money.
I couldn't buy anything.
We're out of clean water.

Julian   We've got none left?

Darren   We're almost out.
We've just got my ration.
I was wondering – should I give it to you, or should I . . .

Julian   You give it to Tara.

Darren   You're sure.

Julian   Of course.

Darren   I thought you would be.
I'll give my ration to Tara.
We'll drink the stuff from the taps
The stuff that rots your brain and eats your belly.

Julian   You don't mind, do you?
Giving up your ration for Tara.

Darren   Me?
Of course not.
Of course I should give up my ration for Tara.
I'd give up anything for –
that's only fitting.
That's only right.

Scene Eight

Tara   He's getting worse.

Darren *doesn't answer.*

Tara   I think he's got a fever.

Darren *doesn't answer.*

Tara   He needs food. Medicine. Clean water, at least.

Darren   There's none here.

Tara   No.
Which is why you have to go and get some /

Darren   / I can't go out.
I went out.

Tara   He's going to die.

Darren   Oh, yes.

Tara   He's going to die unless you do something.

Darren   You go, then.
You go, get medicine, get water.

Tara   Obviously I can't.

Darren   If you can't, how can I?
We're the same.
I took you in, I sheltered you, and now we're the same.

Tara *looks at him.*

Darren   Or is that wrong?

Tara   No, it's right.
We're the same.
And I'd go if I could.
But I can't.
So you have to.

Darren (*looks at her*)   The last time I went out.
I ended up down by the quay.
I saw my reflection.
I saw what I looked like.

Tara   You know.
If Julian could walk, he'd do it.
If you needed water, or medicine
He'd do what needed to be done.
He'd risk it. He'd risk himself.

Darren   I think I risked myself enough when I opened my door, and let you in, and saved your lives.

Tara   You took the exact same risk we've lived with for years.
And we never had a choice.

Darren   Not that you'd have taken it.

Tara   If we had *any* choice, we'd have taken it.

Darren   If you could have chosen to be like us.
To be so much less.

Would you?

Beat.

You see.
Even now.

Tara   But you could choose to be so much more.

Darren (*looks at her*)   At least before you came along
I had my own kind
as clumsy
and mean-spirited

Kelly   and graceless

Darren   and cowardly

Kelly   and shapeless

Darren   and flabby

Kelly   and foul

Darren   as they were.
I had them.
They were mine.
I wasn't ashamed among them.
I am now.

Beat.

Tara   That's a lie.
You told us you'd stopped leaving the house.
You told us you couldn't bear to open the door.
You were ashamed all along.
And you fucking should have been.
Not 'cause of shapeless, or flabby, or clumsy:
But because of death squads, and quarantines, and factories
for the safe disposal of the bodies.
It was when we came, you managed to face them again.
Because you knew you weren't like them.

Darren *looks.*

Tara   Show me you're not like them.

Darren *looks at her. Looks to* **Kelly**.

Kelly   I'd have killed you in a second.
I'd've done exactly the same thing.
If it meant I could really have one of them.
That would be only . . . fitting.
That would be a right thing to do.
So'll all forgive you.
As long as it's not just –
– the same old story:
We turn on each other for want of them.
We chew each other up, for want of them.
And yet to them we're just –
– by-standers, shopkeepers, office dwellers,
fetchers, carriers, runners of errands
Shoulders to cry on, sidekicks, best friends,
But never worthy of serious consideration.
Not in that way.

Beat.

I'll understand.
We all will.

Beat.

Darren   Show me.

Tara *looks at him.*

Darren   Show me I'm better than them.
Show me I'm more.
Show me I'm . . . as much as Julian.

Beat.

Tara   What I remember is:
The precision of it.
His use of angles.
He put his arms round me,
Lifted me off my feet,

Lowered me down to the floor.
I bent at the waist.
I bent so my body was an L-shape.
The bend was at an angle of almost exactly ninety degrees.
He then pushed against my shoulder,
Till my back, my neck, my head were all on the floor.
I was flat against its surface.
He parted my legs at this point.
Still flat against the floor
But parted: the angle was I would say
Fifty degrees.
Then he crouched at one side
Slid his arm under my knees
And lifted them up
So on the horizontal plane my legs stayed parted
At around fifty degrees
But they now were also raised into the vertical plane
The angle of the bend at my knees was I would say
Around a hundred and ten degrees. Maybe a hundred and fifteen.
After that –

Julian (*comes awake*)   Tara.

Tara   I'm here.

Kelly   Did that –
– was she worth it?
Was she worth . . . me?

Julian   Tara.

Tara   I'm here, sweetheart.

Julian   You don't . . . you look different.

Tara (*beat*)   We had to cut my hair. For food.
We had to pull my teeth. For water.

Julian (*beat*)   That'll be it, then.

Tara   But now we're out of water again.
We've got nothing at all left to eat.

Beat.

And Darren doesn't feel
It's appropriate he go out to fetch food and water for us.

Julian *looks from* **Tara** *to* **Darren**.

Darren   I'm more than a fetcher and carrier.

Julian   Of course you are.
I'd go, if I could –
– if I was myself.

Darren (*beat*)   I know.
Tara has explained that to me.
She's helped me see that.

Julian *looks at* **Tara**.

Darren   But you're not yourself.
You're somewhat less.
Whereas I –
– I am somewhat more, it seems.
So I'll go.
I'll go and do what needs to be done.

Julian *approaches* **Tara**. *Reaches out to touch her. Draws back.*

Julian   What's happened to you?

Tara (*beat*)   Nothing.

Julian   What have you done?

Tara *says nothing.*

Darren   He seemed – to flicker.

Tara   I have been protected.
By life, by luck
And since the world started to go to hell,
By you.
I have been protected so long I hoped
It might have made me pure.
And being pure, I hoped –

I hoped I could stay pure in my heart,
No matter what happened to my surface.
Is that right?

Darren   He seemed to flicker.

Julian   Yes, that's right.

Tara   So now if you would hold me
If your arms could map out the world
If your breath could warm the back of my neck
If your fingers could gently stroke my hair.
If you could make it seem like the world loves me.

Julian   Yes, of course.
Yes all that.

Darren   He seemed to flicker and not quite be there.

Julian   Yes, I'll do all that
As soon as I've been out and got us this food and this water.

Tara   What?

Julian   I've been lying in my sick-bed far too long.
I've been letting you cope
I've been letting you get on with things,
And now you've . . . adapted to your surroundings.

Darren   He drags himself up from the bed.

Julian   If you want something done –
– that's fine.

Tara   What I need done is –
– what I need is a moment.
Julian.

Julian   Don't –

Darren   I could –
I could hold you.

Julian (*looks away*)   I'll go and fetch the food, and the
water, and –

– I shouldn't have let you . . .

Tara   Julian.

Darren   He squeezes past her
Coming close but not close enough to touch.
He runs up the stairs.

Tara (*to* **Darren**)   Will you stop him?

Darren   But – this is what he does.
He brings you here.
He delivers you to me.
And when I fail.
When I prove myself not to be enough
He goes and sorts it all out.
Because he – will not fail.
He is proud, and heroic, and strong,
And radiant, and pure
And above all, untainted by shame.
He doesn't exist in the same world as me.
In the same world as us.

Julian   God . . .

Darren   She runs into the hall.

Julian   . . . what a relief to feel the breeze again.

Darren   She takes one step beyond the doorway.

Julian   Sunshine. Sunshine on my skin . . .

Darren   And then she pulls up hard.

Julian   Get out here and feel it, just for a moment.

Darren   She pulls up hard when she sees – the citizens.

Tara   They –
They crowd around him.

Darren   They – are afraid to touch him for a while.

Julian   You see?
You see?

They won't even lay a finger on us.

Darren   A woman reaches out, holds her hand up to his
face –

Tara   – but cannot quite touch him.

Darren   She sees the glow of his cheeks.
She sees something in his eyes.

Tara   She sees her reflection.
She sees what she looks like.

Kelly   She sees herself tiny and twisted.

Darren   And she –

Tara   She reaches out
To fetch herself.
She reaches out with her thin and bony fingers
She reaches deep into his shining eyes.

Darren   He falls.
Face down.

Tara   The circle closes around him.
They kick and stamp
They're treading him into the ground.
Someone comes with paraffin.
They pour it on.
They set it light
And as it burns, they're –

Darren   They're joking.
Joking it's their first whiff of roast meat since rationing
began.
Joking that if the flames leave anything behind, they might
well tuck in.
His arms fly up.
– I can see a ragged hole in the palm of his hand,
Where a stick or a heel has stamped straight through the
charred skin and bone, and come out the other side.
A little kid runs up to the circle, finds his mum amongst the

crowd, curls himself around her leg.
The kid watches for a while.
Then he darts forward, swings his foot back, gives the body
the biggest kick his muscles can manage.
His mum . . . smiles at him, and pats him on the head.

Scene Nine

Darren   What we know now is
You can bear to be touched by me.
Maybe you didn't exactly like it
But I think that was because Julian was still around.
We shouldn't let the uncertainty
Of that first experience
Contaminate future experiences we might have together.

Tara   You dreamed about this. About having one of us.
You dreamed: that one of us would find you charming.
Your need for constant reassurance.
Your whining.
Your inability to dress.
Your awkwardness at table.
We might well.
We might well find that charming.

Darren   I never dreamed of /

Tara   / We might well prefer that to clear eyes and ready
smiles and hearts not filled with hate.

Julian   What is this place?

Kelly *shrugs.*

Julian   Who are you?

Kelly   I – (*Shrugs.*)

Darren   I never dreamed of having one of your kind.
I only dreamed of –
– someone.

And now you're here.
Now you're here to stay.

Tara *looks at him.*

Darren   Tara. No.

Tara   The door swings open.
I step out: my skin seems to crackle and tighten in the
sunshine.
I walk across the street.
I kneel: the pavement is stained with blood and ash.
I reach out. I stroke the ground where he fell.
I wait.
I wait for the punches and kicks.
And . . .
There's a shout behind me.
A tone I recognise.
A cop.
I see the uniform coming for me through the crowd
I see his arm reach inside his jacket,
I hear the crack of the holster coming open
He stops. He takes aim.
I turn to face him.
He looks away: he lowers his gun.
I'm sorry, ma'am, he says.
Just, from a distance, you looked a little like –
He dries up.
I'm sorry, he says. Please, you need to get to high ground.
(*To* **Darren**.) What've you done to me?

Darren   I couldn't make it that the world would love
you.
I've made it that the world won't hate you, instead.

Kelly   I can just make out your face: an outline at first, but
recognisably a human face. I move closer and –

Julian   Your left arm is missing.
Tendons hanging loose.
Your body ends at your belly button. Tubes and organs

hang down like a skirt.
Your jaw is broken. Your mouth ruined.

Kelly   There are scars. Burns all over your face. Your eyes
are gone. Your lips are blisters. Your nose is just a bone.
Tufts of scorched hair poke up from your scalp.
And in your hand, a hole burned right through.

Beat.

Look at us.

Darren   I –
– I saved you.

Kelly   Time begins to pass again.
We know because: a moon appears
and circles the sky.

Julian   A child comes.
A little . . .

Kelly   . . . girl?

Julian   A little girl.

Kelly   And when the moon rises in the sky
She asks where this ball of silver came from,
And where is it going, and can she go there too.

Julian   We tell her the moon is a garden, a heaven,
A home for the world's last treasures
A garden we hid in a stone, and threw up to the sky
To keep it safe when the seas rose.
We tell her how every day the moon comes closer
And soon it will fall and crack open the ground
Water will run again across the bed of the ancient sea
Life will start again, and spread across the land.

Kelly   You stretch up your arm, you uncurl your fist,
The moon is framed by the hole in your palm.
And our little angel shouts in delight, her eyes gleam and
blaze
To see her daddy hold the moon in his hand.

Fags

An early version of *Fags* was presented by Paines Plough at the Bridewell Theatre, London, as part of the Wild Lunch season of new work in June 2001. The cast was as follows:

James   Steve Meo
Liz   Lynn Hunter

Directed by Vicky Featherstone

Fags was first produced in Wales by Slush Theatre at the Aberystwyth Arts Centre, December 2001, with the following cast:

James   Andy Cornforth
Liz   Naomi Jalil

Directed by Andy Cornforth

Although the two pieces stand alone, *Fags* is a companion piece to *Cancer Time*. If the two are performed together, *Fags* should come first, and *Cancer Time* second.

Liz, *late forties, is sitting at a table.* **James**, *late twenties, appears.*

Liz Oh, hello.
I thought you'd gone.

James I've got this one last bone to pick.

Liz Oh . . . *really.*

James Exactly. Exactly.
You're twenty-fours hours from death, but the doctors find a perfect match for your ruined organs. Massive relief.
And then someone walks in and says 'I've got a bone to pick with you' and your heart sinks.
Like – a balloon.

Liz A *balloon?*

James Yeah. Like a balloon. Because –
they start off all cheerful and full of helium and a little kid hanging on to the string wondering how this marvellous silver thing stays up in the sky, and the answer is – it doesn't. It comes down. And it ends up caught on railings or floating on a puddle.
Kid in tears. Loving parent stroke parents in stress, probably wishing they'd stroke she'd been a bit more scrupulous contraceptive-wise.

Liz Where the buggery did I go wrong with you?

James We could churn out a whole series of self-help volumes on that one, couldn't we.

Liz Pay for my retirement.

James Someone's going to have to.
Nice to see you thinking ahead, by the way.

Liz Thanks.

James I imagine it was a lack of scrupulousness, contraceptive-wise.

Liz *looks.*

James   Where you went wrong / with me.

Liz   / So – get it over with.
The sodding bone.

James   Oh, the *sodding* bone.

Liz   Mm.

Beat.

James   There isn't one.
But what a stupid fucking way that is of starting anything.
'I've got a bone to pick with you.'
Gets everyone all defensive and edgy and ready to kick off.
And – you used to do it all the bastard time.

Liz   All the *bastard* time.

James   Actually, yes.

Liz   And you mention that right now 'cause – of what?

James   No particular reason.

Liz   Oh right.

James   Just a note for future reference.

Liz   For the next time I'm dragging up a kid?

James *shrugs.*

Liz   You liar.
You did have a bone to pick.
Yes you did.
The bone you wanted to pick
Was my habit of starting off a discussion
By saying 'I've got a bone to pick with you.'

James   I guess that counts, yeah.

Liz   And you brought it up by using the phrase 'I've got a bone to pick with you.'

Beat.

Were you being ironic, James, when you did that? Is that what you were doing? Or were you just having a go?

James *shrugs.*

Liz   You've learned sod-all from my mistakes, haven't you.

James   Hardly worth you making them, then.
Should've been a bit more scrupulous. Shouldn't you.

Beat.

Liz   Is that what you think? 'Cause that's what I'm thinking now.
I just shouldn't've bothered.
Would've saved everybody a lot of trouble.

James   Mum –

Liz   D'you remember – how you taught me the meaning of irony?

James   And there's a sentence you don't hear every day –

Liz   You don't remember.

James   Almost anything you say after a sentence like that is going to come across as astonishing and profound.

Liz *(considers, then:)*   You were reading the *Beano*. Or – it might have been the *Dandy*. Or the *Eagle*. Or was it – no, it *was* the *Beano*.
Or the – what was that other one called, the – *Victor*? Or – no, no: it was the *Eagle*.

James   Anything except fussing over trivial fucking details that are irrelevant to the point you're actually trying to make.

Liz   No – it *was* the *Dandy*. I remember because you were wearing that little Minnie the Minx badge you had. I think you fancied her, didn't you? Couldn't stand the sight of girls back then, but you didn't mind them if they were in /
cartoons.

James   / Jesus, give me strength.

Liz *smiles.*

James (*smiles back*)   Besides which, Minnie the Minx was in the *Beano*. As any fool knows.

Liz   You were reading this comic – which comic I don't remember, but not to worry, it's irrelevant to the point I'm actually trying to make – and you came across a word you didn't know.

James   'At just nineteen, Corporal Alf Davies made the ultimate sacrifice for King and Country.'

Liz   And you showed it to me; and I didn't know either.

James   'He dived into an enemy machine gun nest that had his men pinned down, clutching the platoon's last hand grenade.'

Liz   You were six years old. And you were asking me words I didn't know.

James   'Corporal Davies took out the machine gun nest but was killed in the explosion.'

Liz   I went into the library the next day and looked it up in the dictionary there –

James   'Ironically, Nazi High Command had surrendered only hours before.'

Liz   And the dictionary said: 'a statement made with the intention of conveying other than that which would ordinarily be conveyed by the meanings of the sentences employed.' And it still didn't seem to make any sense.

James   It was the eighties, mum. It wouldn't have done.

Liz   I remember thinking I'd have to get a dictionary for the house, 'cause then I wouldn't have to tell you I didn't know what words meant; I could just tell you to look them up in the dictionary.

James You got me one for my birthday. I remember asking you what I was having and you said it was something you could do anything and everything with. And I was convinced I was getting a pogo stick.

Liz And I thought: that's what grown-ups do. They say to kids to look things up in the dictionary, 'cause they don't know what half the words mean themselves.
And then I realised – oh Christ. I've got a husband and a kid and I don't know what half the words mean. I must be a grown-up now.

Beat.

Sorry: you were saying?

Beat.

James What d'you call the lodger, now?

Liz I call him Paul, what with that being his name.

James And is Paul around?

Liz His bloody cup is.

James His *bloody* cup.

Liz Wherever you can stand that you can put a cup down on the draining board, from that exact same position you can reach the bloody dishwasher.
But – can he be arsed?

James Doesn't look like it.

Liz Not from the way the cup's – just sitting there on the draining board.

James Gathering dust.

Liz Mmm.

James Growing mould.
Breaking up the clean stainless steel lines of the work surfaces.

Liz   Hardly bloody stainless.

James   You've done your best with it, though. You and the Jif.

Liz   They call it 'Cif' now.
All these years, and suddenly – 'Cif'.
I've defected to Mr Muscle.

James   Not 'Kiff'?

Liz *looks at him.*

James   It's not pronounced 'Kiff'? The new name.

Liz   I don't – think so.

James   But you worry.

Liz   And the *bloody cup* will be there –

James   – getting blood everywhere, which *someone* is going to have to clean up, presumably –

Liz   – all bloody weekend till he gets –

James   – busted out of jail by his drug-lord bosses.

Liz   Back from Calais.
Or the Isle of Man. Or Luton.
Or wherever he's driving his bloody pensioners.

James   So he's *not* around, then.

Liz *looks at him.* **James** *smiles.*

Liz   And he's got all these poncey little toiletries, that he swipes from hotels, littering up the bathroom. And then he's got the cheek to use mine half the time.
And – a shower cap, for God's sake.

James   Interesting you use that word.
'Poncey'.

Beat.

Liz   It is quite a moustache.

James   Christ: how many times?
Bloke with moustache – gay as you like.
A Welsh bloke with moustache – is labouring under the
impression that it helps.
Or possibly – gay as you like.

Liz   It's not the moustache that makes me think. It's –

Liz *and* **James** *smile at each other a little.*

James   . . . the fact that he snogs men? And holds their
hands? And dreams about them when he goes to sleep at
night?

Liz   He's never here. He's always 'round his friend's'.

James   And that's pissing you off because?

Liz   I couldn't care less. Suits me fine.

Beat.

But.

James *waits.*

Liz   What's the point of paying for a room if you're not
going to use it?
Except to store your bloody underwear.
Which he folds, by the way.

James   You should have said.

Liz   Well, and then *with* the moustache.

James   So, essentially, your lodger –
Sucks cock.

Liz *slaps his hand.*

James   I mean I'm proud.
Who'd've thunk it?
And you ten years ago. Married to –

They try to remember.

Liz   Your dad?

James   And now: a cock-sucking lodger.

Liz   Will you stop –

James   – saying 'cock-sucking'?

Liz   Yes.

James   And 'cock-sucker'?

Liz   Mm.

James   And: 'great big huge cock and balls' –

Liz   – that's it. We're changing the subject.

James   OK.

Beat.

You're looking a bit tense, Mum.
You all right?

Liz   I'm fine.

James   You don't need your inhaler?

Liz   I could've sworn I just said I was fine.

James   Asthma not playing you up lately, then?

Liz   No.

James   That's good to hear.
I worry, you know.

Liz   I worry.
I was always worried, with you.
I was right to be, wasn't I.

They stare at each other.

It was a struggle, though, getting you to read at all.

Beat.

James   I'm sure it was.

Liz   I had to force you.
Three pages of Peter and Jane a night.
Do you remember?

James   Of course.

Liz   Do you?
D'you remember you used to scream and cry and call me all
sorts?
The end of that summer, though, you went back to school,
and you could read better than anyone in the class.
You remember the look on that teacher –

James   Mrs Pearce.

Liz   – the look on her face, that Mrs Pearce?

James   Yes. I remember.

Liz   You never stopped then. Then it was I couldn't get
new books fast enough. You went through all the Peter and
Janes and straight on to –

James   – the Famous Five.

Liz   But you didn't like getting books from the library. You
didn't like having to give them back, did you? You wanted
to keep them for yourself / forever.

James   / Do you remember – when you thought I was
gay?

Liz   Well –
– your mate was.

Smiles to herself.

It was the eighties.
What did we know?
We ate pub grub.
And we liked it.

James   He's dead now.
My mate. Who was gay.

Liz   No.

James   AIDS.

Beat.

From sucking loads and loads and loads of cocks.

Liz (*looks at him, then:*)   You *bastard.*

James (*smiles*)   You – *mother to a bastard.*

They sit and smile at each other for a bit.

Liz   I didn't know you could get it from just –

James *dares her to continue.*

Liz   From oral . . . activities.

James   You thought – there had to be an actual
ejaculation into an anal passage and then sperm penetrating
a rupture in the anal passage, and settling down in the blood
stream.

Liz (*steels herself a little*)   Mm.

James   Well, apparently not.
If there's some kind of cut or tear in the lining of your
mouth. Perhaps caused by – a bit of muesli.
And then your mouth gets flooded by a great wad of come.

Liz *hides her head in her hands.*

James   You OK, Mum?
You all right with this topic of conversation?

Liz   You lying little sod.

James   So what happens is, the come floods your mouth
right to the brim. And it finds the cut or tear before you
have time to gobble it all down –

Liz   – OK.

Beat.

OK, you lying little sod.
I knew you had a bone to pick /

James   / What's happened to the lounge?
The smell.

Liz   Oh, Christ –

James   Oh, Christ, she says.

Liz   It's – alpine fresh.

James   It bloody is that.
I walked in, I was expecting Austrians.

Liz *says nothing.*

James   Austrians in fucking lederhosen.
Or Christmas at least.

Beat.

Liz   I have got a new – string to my bow.

James *says nothing.*

Liz   I have taken –

James *says nothing.*

Liz   . . . to buying myself some little treats every now and
again.

James *says nothing.*

Pause.

Liz *gets up and walks off.*

She comes back with something concealed in each hand.

She sits.

James *watches her.*

Liz *reaches a hand out and puts something on the table.*

James *looks at it.*

James   It's –

Liz   . . . a lighter.

James   A crappy little lighter.

Liz   Five for a pound. From the cheap shop.

James   I've heard lighters from the cheap shop blow up.
In your face or your hands.
People's lives have been – literally ruined.

Liz *says nothing.*

James   What d'you need a lighter for, Mum? What d'you
need *five* lighters for?

Liz *reaches out her other hand and leaves something on the table.*

James *looks down.*

James   What's that about?

Liz   It's mostly about

Beat.

that I've put all this weight on.

James   All this weight? Where the fuck's all this weight?

Beat.

Liz   You can't see it.
'Cause I dress defensively.
But it's there.
And I have to carry it round.

James   You liar.
What's Mar say?

Liz   Mar doesn't say anything.

James   She doesn't say 'Mum, the lounge smells like
Austrians and where the fuck did that come from?'

Liz   No.

James   She'd be gutted.

Liz   If she knew.

Beat.

James   She probably does know.
She probably does know, she probably just doesn't say
anything. She probably just – keeps it to herself.
And carries it round with her.

Liz   Don't you dare lecture me
About causing upset to Mared.

Beat.

It's not like I'm back on sixty a day, for Christ's sake.

James   Fifty-nine and a half, though?

Liz   It's just if we go out for a drink after work.
And someone's passing them around.
Just socially.

James   Just socially.

Liz   Yeah.

James   You go out twice a year.

Liz   Yeah, so it's not like –

James   – Christmas and – at least one other occasion, in
any twelve-month period.

Liz   Pat's birthday, usually.

James   So how come – the chemical scouring of the
lounge?

Beat.

Liz   Well, I mean. When it started –

James   When it *started*. There's history to this, then,
already.

Liz   It started with just going out, on those rare occasions that I ever do. And people are passing them round. And you can hardly take if you haven't got any to offer back, can you?

James   You can.
From some people.

Beat.

Liz   So you buy a pack of ten, just to have some to offer back.
You come home with a few left, and the packet in your handbag.
It's Friday night. There's crap-all on the telly. You're working your way through your box of dry white.
So –

James   And how often would you say this happens?

Liz   Just – the once a week. Just the Friday.
To start with.

James   I thought to start with, it was just twice a year. When you went out.

Liz   Then I got into the habit of buying a pack of ten. On a Friday. To offer back to people. And just finishing them off at home.

Beat.

James   On a Friday.

Liz   Mm.

James   Just on a Friday.

Liz   Do you have any idea how crap Saturday night telly is these days?

James   Friday and Saturday, then.

Liz *looks.*

James   Every night, then.

Liz   You're going to go mad now, aren't you.

James   No.
Not at all.
Because: I understand completely.
What you're describing, you and the fags.
Of course I understand.

Liz   I don't want to hear about it.

James   Of course you don't.

Liz   It's just – till I get this weight off. Then I'll stop.
I just don't feel like me at the moment.
I'll get back to being me.
And then I'll give up again.

James   You know what a completely bullshit thing that is
to say, don't you?

Beat.

And how can you even afford it? It's like what, four quid for
twenty now.

Liz   I afford it – with my bloody wages.
Plus. You go down the shop, and you ask have they got any
cheap cigarettes. And they have them under the counter.
From France.

James   Mother of two.
One-time Tory voter.
And now – receiver of smuggled goods.

Liz   – it's just.
I like it. I really like it. I like smoking. And someone offered
me a fag and I didn't want to say no.

Beat.

I thought back to why I started saying no: and it was
because of Mar and her asthma, and you going on and on
about the smell on your clothes.

James *looks at her.*

Liz   I never used to smoke in your room, I never used to smoke when I was doing the ironing, I always had the window open when I smoked in the lounge and you still went on that you could smell the smoke on your clothes. And I remember you crying for hours and hours one day about it and I just thought: bugger it. Too much bloody hassle. I'll give up.

Beat.

James   I remember the day you stopped. I'd flushed your last pack down the toilet.
You were going to go mad; and then you didn't. You turned round and walked out the house.
I ran after you, and you said you were just going down the shops. I begged you not to go and you said did I want any sweets.
I said no I didn't want any sweets, I just wanted you not to go.

Beat.

The moment the car was out of the drive, Steve came up to my room, saying if I didn't stop upsetting you, he'd smash my fucking face in, and I'd have to go and live with my dad.

Liz *looks.*

James   Face smashed in *and* going to live with my dad.
You'd think either one would be punishment enough.
Not for that fucker, though.
He wanted to get rid, didn't he.
But then, as it happened.
Six months later, Christmas Day, and there he is coming into my room again. For – the second time ever.
Only now with a mugful of vodka.
And he's crying, and telling me you've asked him to go.
But he's always gonna love me and Rich, no matter what.
And I remember thinking:

Vodka.
Vodka, in a mug, filled right up to the brim.
I should try some of that.
Smash *my* fucking face in. And get rid of *me*.

Beat.

Liz   The thing is.
You wouldn't stop, love.
I didn't know what more to say to you.

James *picks up her gaze.*

Liz   You just kept on and on and on about it.
You were driving me spare.
And so Steve,
I asked Steve if there was anything he could do.
He said yes there was,
He said he'd have a word with you –

James *looks away.*

Liz   In the end, it's just – it's just embarrassing being told you stink like an ashtray, isn't it?

Beat.

You just went on and on.

Beat.

You wouldn't *stop*.

Beat.

James   No.

Beat.

Liz   So I stopped.
I gave up my fags.

Beat.

But you're not around any more.

James   No. I'm not.

Liz   And Mared I hardly see.
And so –
I like it. I like having a fag of an evening.
I'm here, night after night jumping between soap operas.
With my box of dry white.
And my appreciation of irony.
And my cock-sucking lodger.
And he's hardly ever around.
And sometimes I find I've gone in and switched on his telly
so there's that little murmuring from his room.
Like there was when it used to be your room.
And it helps, a bit. Just to have a fag.

They hold each other's gaze.

James *looks away.*

Liz *opens the cigarette packet.*

It's empty.

Liz   I'm just gonna pop down Spar.

James   It wasn't the fucking smell. It wasn't the fucking
smell of the smoke.
It was – you sitting there
Telling us how you were gonna get a little cottage by the sea
And that one day we'd sleep to the sound
Of pebbles crackling in the tide.

Liz   I'd've gone to the Post Office and Val would've let me
have the child benefit a couple of days early.
Then I'd go to the butcher and buy six sausages.
Eggs from Nanny. Spuds from the garden.
Then you'd bring one of your mates home for tea.
You and Mared and your mate would sit down and have
egg and chips. And two sausages each.
I'd tell you I was having my tea later, after you'd gone to
bed.

And I'd have a fag in the garden, 'cause I didn't like
smoking round you when you were eating.

Beat.

I wonder if you'll be here,
When I get back.

James   You should've said.

Liz   No. I shouldn't.
I didn't mind any of that.
I'd watch you through the kitchen window – I'd watch you
smiling, blabbering away with your mate.
And the fags keep your appetite down anyway.
But you, six years old and looking up at me and asking me a
word and you're so sure that I will know –
– and I don't.

Beat.

I go down to Spar for my fags
And when I get back, I usually find
I've gotten a four-pack, like I always would
Just in case you dropped by.
I end up drinking them myself, these days,
If Paul doesn't have them.

James   I just wanted to do something,
You know? See a few / things

Liz   / Of course I fuckin' know.
Everyone knows. Everyone feels like that, love.
They feel it all the time, no matter what happens.

Beat.

I'm getting quite a taste for Stella now, as it happens.

James   If I'd had kids.
Mum, if I'd had a kid.
If I had given you a granddaughter –

Liz But, love – you didn't.
You didn't do that.
So just let me
Hang on to the fags, and
I'll see you again, all right.

Cancer Time

Cancer Time was originally produced in Welsh as *Amser Canser* in February 2003 by the Royal Welsh College of Music and Drama in association with Sgript Cymru. The cast was as follows:

Mared   Mared Swain
Iola   Iola Hughes

Directed by Jamie Garven

This translation was first produced at Theatre 503 by Caird Company and Theatre 503 on 7 September 2004. The cast was as follows:

Mared   Karen Paullada
Iola   Tonya Smith

Directed by Alex Clifton
Designed by Paul Burgess
Lighting by Ben Polya
Sound by Phil Hewitt

Scene One

Inside.
Two desks. On each desk, a keyboard and headset.

Mared *takes a while to decide which desk she wants.*
She spots something under one of the desks.
She pulls the hidden thing out.
The thing is a big box: a box wrapped in exciting paper, with glitter and ribbons.

Mared *hears someone else arriving. She sits quickly and hides the box.*

Iola *sees* **Mared***; smiles at her.* **Mared** *looks away.*

Iola *goes to sit at the other desk.*
They both put their headsets on.
And take a deep breath.
And fall asleep.

Scene Two

Outside.

Mared*'s sitting on her own. She's reading* Heat *magazine.*

Mared   'At the MTV Awards, Jack Osbourne couldn't resist sitting on Britney's lap.'
Pus-filled scrubber.

Iola *arrives. She's carrying a packet of fags.*

Iola *sees* **Mared***. She walks over to join her.*

Mared *realises she's being watched.*

She carries on reading, without acknowledging **Iola***.*

Iola *sits some distance away from* **Mared***.*

She looks at **Mared***.*

Mared *doesn't respond.*

Iola *looks away.*

She sees something really exciting and impressive.

Iola   Fucking –

She pulls up.

Fuck me, that had to hurt.

Beat.

Did you see that?

Mared *ignores her.*

Iola   Did you see that kid?

Mared (*without looking up*)   Yes, I saw him.

Iola (*moving to sit next to* **Mared**)   Just I asked if you'd seen him
And you said

Beat.

Not a lot.

Mared *looks at her.*

Iola   You mind me sitting here?

Mared   Fuck me, no, not in the slightest.

Iola (*beat*)   I was sitting with those lot over there but
I think I've pissed them off a bit.
So I thought I might wander over here.
Talk to you.
'Cause you're new, aren't you.
I haven't had time to piss you off, yet.

Mared *looks at her.*

Iola *shuts up.*

Iola   See, I'm the kind of person
That can't abide a silence.
If there's a silence, I like to fill it up.

Mared   With ceaseless chatter.

Iola   Or perhaps with a memory game.
Or a card game.
Or by listening to music.
Or – with people. I love people.
I love – getting to know people.

Beat.

All their ins and outs.

She waits for **Mared** *to respond.* **Mared** *does not.*

Iola   What's your story, then?
What d'you like?

Mared   I'm fairly fond of being left in peace.

Iola   Really?

(*She considers.*)

Oh no, I don't like that at all.
'Cause when you're left in peace,
That's when you start to, you know –

Beat.

Look into yourself.

At this **Mared** *looks up.*

Iola   I'm not so fond of guessing games, I've gotta say.
With guessing games there's always that
Random element. And randomness just puts me in mind of
Car crashes. And car crashes, and all forms of
Sudden, unpredictable death really
Are a big source of anxiety for me.

Beat.

I think what I love most about smoking
– aside from the sheer glamour of it –
Is that it gives you cancer.
Because the thought that cancer is

Very slowly, but very definitely coming for me
Really helps take the edge
Off my anxiety about sudden, unpredictable death.

They sit. Silence.

D'you think he's OK?

Mared (*beat: she gives up reading*)   We'll see now.
If he starts screaming inside a couple of seconds
More than likely he's fine.
If he doesn't . . .

They watch for a while.

Mared   You see? His lungs are all right.

They watch for a little more.

And if there was anything wrong with his heart
The blood wouldn't be –
– exploding out of him like that.

Mared *goes back to her magazine.*

Iola *tries again.*

Iola   You want a / fag?

Mared   / No thanks.

Silence.

Iola *fiddles with the fag packet.*

The fiddling gets on **Mared**'s *nerves.*

Iola *realises the fiddling is getting on* **Mared**'s *nerves.*
And so she stops.
And so she starts again.

Mared   You know why the skaters do it, all that
Viciously dangerous jumping?

Iola *shakes her head.*

Mared   They are – slaves to the power

Of music.
They can't help themselves.

Iola *goes to speak.*
Changes her mind.

Mared   You know they say sculpture
Is frozen music.

Iola   How does that work?

Mared   If you let your eyes lose focus
You find you can see
The concrete start to shift.

Iola *squints.*

Mared   The voices start to shift
Under the face of the concrete.

Iola *squints more.*

Mared   And that is what the skaters feel.
That's what draws them in.
That's what makes them ignore the pain and the peril:
The music of the concrete.
Can you see it? The frozen music.

Iola   Not really, no.

Mared   Well, you just keep trying.

Iola *keeps squinting.*

Mared *goes back to her magazine.*

Iola *squints, trying to see the music.*

Eventually, **Iola** *feels a bit of an idiot, and gives up.*
She takes a fag from the packet.
She brings it to her mouth.
She sits with the fag between her lips for a moment, without lighting it.
She pulls the fag from her mouth.

Iola   All I wanted was a chat, for fuck's / sake

Mared   / Now, those skaters over there –
– d'you see them?

Iola   Of course I fucking see them.

Mared   Those lot are hardline modernists.
They say 'no' to melody and harmony.
They insist the virtues of music as we have known it
Nowadays serve only to tranquillise the mind
And help us not face the reality of hell on earth
Which has been observed in Auschwitz, Dresden, Nagasaki,
Cambodia, NYC, the Gaza Strip
– the list goes literally on.
So they skate along the steps, down the railings, up the kerbs
And when they fall
Then, they face a hard reality.
The reality of concrete
Colliding with nosebone.

Beat.

But these kids by here
These foolish fucking – romantics.
They skate on sculpture.
They skate – on music.

Beat.

That has been frozen.

Beat.

In concrete.

Iola *looks away.*
She watches the skaters for a spell.
She puts her cigarette back in its packet.
She watches the skaters for a spell longer.

Iola   I thought that was architecture.
All that stuff about frozen music.

Mared   Architecture, sculpture,
Same fuckin thing, isn't it.

Iola   I don't think it fucking is.

Mared *looks at her.*

Mared   It's all rendering brute physical matter
Into a pleasing visual form.

Iola   Except that sculpture's entirely about the visual and tactile
Interest of the finished piece,
Whereas with architecture there's an inherently
Functional aspect to the work, isn't there.

Mared   Sculpture has a function.

Iola   Like what?

Mared   It looks nice.

Iola   Architecture has a practical function
Aside from the purely aesthetic.

Mared   Sculpture can have a practical function.

Iola   I say again – like fucking what?

Mared (*beat*)   An ice sculpture of a man, at a party,
Where you pour the booze in his mouth
And it trickles down inside him
And comes out of his cock, nicely chilled.

Iola *thinks about this.*

Mared *goes back to her magazine.*

Iola   Can I read your copy of *Heat*
When you're finished?

Mared *gives up, hands over the magazine.*

Mared   You go right a-fucking-head, love.

Scene Three

Inside.

Iola *and* **Mared** *are at their desks.*
They're sleeping, collapsed over their keyboards.

Slowly, **Mared** *sits up.*

She checks that **Iola** *is still asleep.*

Mared *takes out the big exciting box.*
She looks at it for a bit.
Then tears off the wrapping paper and opens the box.
She looks inside.
She sees something.
From the box, she takes out – a smaller box.
Smaller in size, but with even more ribbons, bows and fancy things . .

Scene Four

Outside.

Mared *is sitting on her own, reading.*

Iola *appears. She's got a packet of fags.*

Iola *walks towards* **Mared**.

Mared *looks up at her.*
Looks away.

Iola *sits down.*
They watch the skaters for a bit.

Iola   You wanna fag?

Mared   I don't actually smoke.

Iola   Seriously?

Mared   I am just *so* serious.

Iola   You come out for a fag break

Every half an hour.

Mared   So do you.

Iola   I need a fag, don't I.
You're just skiving

Mared   It's the principle of the thing.

Iola   What fucking principle?

Mared   The principle that
The more time I spend out of that fucking office
The longer I'll hold out before going
Finally fucking mad.

Beat.

Iola   See, I think that's cheating.

Mared   Oh, Christ, well I'd better stop now, then . . .

Iola   We are allotted lunchtime 'cause we need
A midday stiffener to survive the afternoon.
We are allotted toilet breaks because
At some point in the day, we're going to need
A good cry, and
We're allotted fag breaks
So we can work up
A nice mid-life cancer, give ourselves
A bit of light at the end of the tunnel.
Taking fag breaks if you're not
Actually trying to catch cancer,
It's just taking the piss out of the system.

Mared   Feel free to report me to your team leader.

Iola   I would, but he's just ducked in the bogs.
For a wank.

Silence.

So . . . what was it that attracted you
To this line of work?

Mared   The money.

Iola   I'll have to remember that.
'The money.'
That's dead fucking / clever.

Mared   / I took this job because
They wouldn't let me in the army.

Iola   Ah . . .

Mared   What?

Iola   So much becomes clear . . .
You don't need to worry: it's fine.

Mared *looks at her.*

Iola   No, I mean that. It's really all right.
I won't say a thing.

Mared   What are you on?

Iola   But if you do choose to
Reveal your same-sex orientation
To the rest of your colleagues then
You can count on my support.

Mared   Oh, fuck off . . .

Iola   And rest assured, the company has
A very progressive take on
All the relevant equality issues.

Mared   I'm not a fucking lesbian 'cause I
Wanted to go in the army.

Iola   Are you sure?
'Cause I do get that vibe off you.
A little bit.

Mared   I wanted to go in the army
So I could fucking kill people
And get paid for it.

Iola   Right.

Mared   That's not to say I wouldn't kill people
Even if I wasn't getting paid for it.
I'd just have to find
Some other source of income.

Iola   That's . . . interesting.

Mared   It is interesting, I think.

Iola   Interesting and
Not a little psychotic.

Mared   Well I don't know.
Who's really the more dangerous?
The person who's wound up, tense,
Pushed to the limit by the stresses of
Contemporary urban living?
Or the person who is calm, placid, sated
Having just indulged in a really
Uninhibited killing spree?
I mean, take you, for example.

Iola   Me?

Mared   You're a bag of nerves. You're a time bomb.
You're disaster footage waiting to happen.
You're a –

She can't think what.

– all this popping out for a fag every five minutes.
And the ceaseless chatter. And the rough sex
With strangers in alleyways.

Iola   I do not fuck strangers in alley/ways

Mared   / So imagine this.
You've had the day from hell.
Middle-class clientele screaming down the line.
The heat has soared to pensioner-snuffing levels.
There's been no Coke in the machine, just Dr Bastard
Pepper,
And you're that bit pre-menstrual, say.

How'd you cope with that?

Iola   Retreat to the pub for a quiet litre of vodka.

Mared   What if, instead, you got to work off your
frustration
Running round some foreign desert
Shooting Third World people in their faces?

Iola   I don't know. I'm not too sure about that.

Mared   What's not to be sure about?

Iola   I don't think you're supposed to call them
Third World people any more. I think they're people
From the world that's developing.

Mared   Third World, developing world,
Could you forget about the semantics, and
Concentrate on the killing?

Iola *considers.*

Iola   I think the first time I'd feel maybe
A second of doubt about what I was doing
But once that second was done, I suspect
The exhilarating roar of my SA80 assault rifle on automatic-
full
And the hideous chorus of all the half-developed people
screaming
And the thump, thump, thump of bodies hitting the ground
Would drown out the bleatings of my flabby Western
conscience.

Mared   Blind, paralysed, puppies tied to rocks
Are harder to drown than the bleatings of
A Western conscience, love.

Iola   I'd imagine the health benefits
Would be considerable. Because in any
Mass slaughter situation, there's always gonna be a few
Who'll try and make a run.

Mared   Kids, especially, will try that.

Iola   Well, it's in their nature.

Mared   Little scamps . . .

Iola   And rounding them all up would provide
An aerobic workout of the most health-giving kind.
Shitloads of adrenaline and endorphins would be
Released into the blood,
And would fight off the energy dip
That tends to hit in the mid-afternoon
And so often prevents one
From hitting one's sales targets
By half past the five every day.

Mared   Plus, in the longer term,
After slaying half-developed people
On the far side of the Earth
Everyday life right here seems almost – endurable.

Iola   I'm gonna have to think about all that.
And then possibly learn to work a gun.

Silence.

Mared   So . . . does wanting to go into the army
Generally mean that you're gay?

Iola   Generally it's fancying people of the same
Sex as you that means you're gay.

Mared   'Cause my brother went into the army,
And I asked him why and
I didn't believe a word he told me.

Iola   He didn't just want to kill
Some of the world's poorest people, and get paid for it?

Mared   No, actually. In stark contrast to that,
He said he wanted to travel the world,
Encounter different societies and cultures,
Learn a trade, aside from cost-efficient killing,
Take part in peace-keeping, nation-building
And related humanitarian activities, and

Generally do something with his life.

Iola   Do something . . .

Mared   With his life. Yeah.

Iola   Is he a very . . . loving kind of boy?

Mared *looks at her.*

Iola   Is he a bit slow?

Mared   Not ordinarily.
And I'm wondering now,
If it's some sort of gay thing.

Iola   Pity if it is.
I like a man in uniform.

Mared   Tell you what, once he gets back
I'll ask him: James, are you a gayer,
'Cause if you're not there's this girl at my work
Who'll let you do her, but only up an alleyway
Against a burned-out car.

Iola   That happened *once*.
And it wasn't with a stranger.

Mared   Nobody's a stranger,
Once they've bought you a second drink.

Iola   No. And a double counts as two drinks,
If you're in a hurry.

Mared   Which you always are.

Iola   Which I often am, yeah.

Scene Five

Inside.
The two girls are sleeping at their desks.

Mared *opens an eye. Makes sure* **Iola** *is still asleep.*

She gets out the big box, puts it on her desk.
She pulls out the smaller box.
She waits for a moment.
Then she opens the smaller box.
In it, she finds an envelope.
A golden envelope.

Scene Six

Outside.

The sun is very strong today.
Iola *arrives.*
She takes a moment to settle herself – taking her cardigan off, spreading it like a blanket on the ground, lying down on it.

Mared *arrives.*

She sees **Iola***.*

Mared   All right?

Iola   Hiya.

Mared *goes to sit a little way off, on her own.*

Iola   Oh, for fuck's sake . . .

Mared *stops.*
She comes and sits next to **Iola***.*
She takes a moment to settle herself.
And then they relax.

Mared   So . . . what do you do here?

Iola   Out *here?*

Mared   In there. In the office?

Iola (*considers*)   I don't remember.

Mared   Have you been here long?

Iola   Two minutes.

Mared   Have you been working here long?

Iola   Ummm . . . I don't remember.

Mared   You gonna stay here long?

Iola   Don't remember.

Mared *considers.*

Mared   What did you dream about last night?

Iola   I can't tell you that!

Mared   Mm.

Beat.

I had a dream that was really, really . . . special.

Iola (*beat*)   When?

Mared   Three days ago.

Iola   Fantastic.

Mared   It was *wholly* fantastic.
I dreamed the world was exactly like it is now.
Except that the language 'Welsh' had died out
In the year sixteen hundred and seventy-five.

Iola   No . . .

Mared   Yes.

Iola   What was it like?

Mared   It was –
– oh my God . . .

Iola   Was it?

Mared   It was just . . .

Shakes her head.

Iola   Oh, wow . . .

Mared   It's upsetting me now just thinking about –

Iola   – the beauty of it?

Mared   Don't, please…

They consider the beauty of it for a moment.

And the faces on the kids . . .

Iola   Were they chuffed?

Mared   Chuffed?
Fuck off . . .

Iola   Sorry. Stupid question . . .

Mared   Chuffed? They were fuckin . . .

Iola   Really, really chuffed?

Mared   Talk about shining in the eyes.
Talk about voices lifted in joy.
Talk about confidence in their cultural hinterland.
Were they fucking chuffed?

Iola   Sorry.

Mared   You're sorry? I had to live through it
And then wake up to the pitiless reality
Of a bleak and hungover morning.
A morning in which the language 'Welsh' still exists,
And I, incredibly, speak it.

Iola   That's gotta hurt.

Mared   Like a bastard.
And you know the first thing I thought?

Iola *tries to imagine.*

Mared   Those fuckin English.
If they needed a language exterminating,
We'd do it for them, and we'd do the job properly,
Not leave it all half-killed and grizzling. Lazy bastards.

Iola   I don't even think it's about laziness.
I think it's about malice.

Mared   You think – they left us like this deliberately?

Iola   Of course. If we didn't have this
Half-rotted language to prop up, the Welsh nation'd be
Bestriding the world like a fuckin cultural colossus by now.

Mared   I hadn't thought it about it like that.

Iola   Not many people have.

Mared   They've just deliberately left us all backward.

Iola   And tribalistic.

Mared   And inward-looking.

Iola   And so, *so* parochial.

Silence.

Mared   I don't even like speaking the language 'Welsh'.

Iola   Christ, who does?

Mared   It's just clinging to a relic of an age
That's long since past. It's just
Sentimentality. And I don't feel
There is any place for sentimentality,
Not in a truly modern Britain living under
The constant threat of apocalyptic terrorism.

Iola   We must love it.

Mared   We love the language 'Welsh'?

Iola   Must do.

Mared   Well if we do, it's an abusive love.

Iola   It's a destructive love.

Mared   It's a love that certainly dares not
Pronounce its own name.

Iola   What I've found, Mared,
Is that if you look into it closely enough,
If you really scrutinise your motives and

And you're really, painfully honest
With yourself, you will find that you love and speak
The language 'Welsh'
Because you are a racist.
Just as everyone who opts to speak
A language other than English
Is, ultimately, a racist.

Mared   Well, good God.

Iola   In fact, I believe God created languages other than
English, simply in order to test us.

Mared   How does that work?

Iola   Those who wish to embrace all humanity, speak
English,
Those who do not . . .

Mared   See, I would never've thought I was a racist.
I'll eat food from anywhere.

Iola   Don't worry, though: it's not your fault.
It is the fault of the English,
Who got us in this state in the first place.

Mared   English bastards.

Iola   English fuckers.

Mared (*beat*)   Great big fuckers.

Iola   Great big English fuckers.

Mared   Great, big, English fuckers . . .

Iola   Great big English fuckers I have known . . .

Mared   Oh, don't.

Iola   Oh, God.

Mared   Oh, please . . .

They consider the greatness of English fuckers for a moment.

Iola   I went out with a boy once.

A boy – from Bir-mingem.

Mared   Bir-mingem?

Iola   Bir-mingem City.

Mared   Where's that?

Iola   Fuck knows.
I wanted him to come to Spain with me.

Mared   OK.

Iola   He wouldn't.
He wanted to stay home and look after his mum.
In Bir-mingem.

Mared   Is there a place for that kind of sentimentality in
modern Britain?
I think not.

Iola   So I said – look.
I know your mum's important to you
But – come on.
She's going to pop it.
Maybe not today. Maybe not tomorrow.
But sometime in the decades to come, she's gonna croak.
So stop wasting your fucking time on her.
Come to Spain with me
And I'll shag your fucking brains out.

Mared   Well, done you.

Iola   But he said – 'No.
I'm staying home to look after me old mum.'
And I said – how can you be so . . . introverted –

Mared   – inward-looking –

Iola   – tribalistic –

Mared   – primitive –

Iola   – parochial –

Mared   – *racist.*

Iola   Well . . . *Exactly.*

Mared   So he was a racist against Spaniards?

Iola   Obviously I accused him of being a racist again
Spaniards.
He very much poo-pooed the idea.

Mared   That's a shitty thing to do.

Iola   I said to him, what's the problem with Spaniards?
What've they ever done to you?
And he said – 'Nothing.
I just love me old mum.'

Mared   Did you chuck?

Iola   Yeah, but I managed to swallow it all back down
Without too much spillage.
I said to him – the world is more than you and your old
mum.
You can't waste your energy and – *your money*
Postponing the inevitable for some relic of an age that has
Long since gone.

Mared   What did he say?

Iola   He just started crying.

Mared   Wuss.

Iola   And I realised what was up.
He wasn't a racist against the Spaniards.
He was a racist against
Everyone in the world.
Except for his old mum, obviously.
And since then, I've noticed:
People who say they love people, or things. They always
turn out
To be racists, in the end.

They relax again.

I've remembered what I'm doing here now.

Mared   Yeah?

Iola   It goes something like –
So can I interest you in purchasing a Gasguard health check
for your boiler, oven or other gas appliance, madam?

Mared   No. You can't.

Iola   A snip at eighty quid plus VAT.

Mared   No thanks.

Iola   Yeah. Like that.
It goes exactly like that.

Mared   That's . . .

Iola   Isn't it?

Beat.

Mared   D'you think
That if we had anything to give a fuck about
Or anything to actually do
We wouldn't need to talk
Such endless fucking shite the whole time?

Iola (*thinks about it*)   Do you want to hear
What I dreamed about last night?

Mared   I'm gagging for the details.

Iola   I dreamed I was one of the luckiest people to live,
ever.

Mared   You dreamed . . . you shagged me?

Iola   I dreamed I was living
In one of the most perfect lands
That had existed on the earth, ever.
Our wise men and ladies understood more of the world
Than any other wise men or ladies who'd tried
To understand the world, ever.
We had the power to solve all the world's problems:
To feed everyone, to educate everyone,

To make sure everyone had a place to stay,
And then to live in peace, and explore inner and outer space together
Forever, and ever, and ever.

Mared   Amen.

Iola   Yeah.

Mared   And what was it like, living your amazing brilliant life?

Iola (*beat*)   It was possible to survive,
By going straight from the job to the pub every night
And then drinking myself into a state of semi-consciousness
So that the hangover the morning after would fuck up half my brain
And make the tedium of my existence half-bearable.

Mared   OK.

Iola   Well, exactly.

Mared   And what did you say, when you woke up?

Iola   I said 'Oh, my God.
Oh, my fucking God.
Thank fuck for that.'

Mared   Mmm.

Iola   Or I take it that I'll say
Something along those lines
Whenever I finally do wake up.

Iola *settles.*
Relaxes back into the sun.
Leaves **Mared** . . . *alone.*

Mared *gets up.*
She goes back to her desk.
She puts the big box on her desk.
She takes the small box out of the big box.
She takes the golden envelope out of the small box.

She hesitates.
She opens the golden envelope.
Inside the envelope, she finds a card.
The card is black.
She opens the card.
She reads the card.

She yelps like she's been hit.

She puts the card into her pocket.

Scene Seven

Outside.

Mared *is sitting on her own.*
She's sitting very quietly.

Iola *appears.*
She watches **Mared** *for a bit.*
She moves slowly towards **Mared**.
She stops near **Mared**, *without sitting.*
Mared *doesn't acknowledge her presence.*
Iola *starts to say something.*
She changes her mind.
She waits, without sitting.
They are perfectly still.

After a spell, **Mared** *half-looks at* **Iola**, *without meeting her eyes.*
Then she looks away again.
Iola *waits for* **Mared** *to say something.*
Mared *stays silent.*
Iola *goes and sits some distance from* **Mared**.

Silence.

Iola *gets up. She makes to leave.*
As she passes near **Mared**, *she stops.*
She turns to **Mared**.
She hesitates, waiting for **Mared** *to tell her to stay or to leave.*
Mared *says nothing.*

Iola *tries to find something useful to say.*
She can't.

Iola *goes and sits next to* **Mared**.
They sit in silence.

After a while, **Mared** *puts her head in her hands.*
Iola *moves nearer to her.*
She raises her hand.
She places her hand on **Mared***'s shoulder.*
Mared *is absolutely still.*
Iola *pulls her hand back.*
Mared *sits up straight again.*
She moves slightly further away from **Iola**.

Iola *watches* **Mared** *move.*
She considers.
She stands.
She turns away.
She stops.
She turns back to **Mared**.
She watches **Mared** *for a moment.*

Iola   Do you want me to just go?

Iola *waits to see if* **Mared** *will react.*
Mared *stays silent.*

Iola   Would you rather not talk about it?

She watches **Mared** *for a moment.*

Iola   Do you want me to just leave you in peace?

Mared *says nothing.*

Iola   Do you want me to just –

Mared *sits, silent and still.*

Iola *sits down next to her.*

Scene Eight

Outside.

Mared *is sitting on her own*

Iola *appears.*
She watches **Mared** *for a bit.*
She walks over towards her.
Mared *looks up.*

Iola   I wasn't expecting to see you in today.

Mared   Sorry to disappoint.

Iola *sits down.*

Mared   There was – a real bitch on the phone with me this morning.

Iola   Was there?

Mared   Yeah, she was just –

Beat.

She was dead fucking funny.

Iola   Was she?

Mared   You should've been there.

Iola   What was she saying?

Mared (*looks at her, then:*)   Just the same stuff as ever, you know.

Iola   The same stuff as ever. And that was funny?

Mared   Her voice, I think, was what made her funny. She wasn't so much saying funny things, just –

Iola   Her voice?

Mared   It was the way she said things that was funny. More than the things she said.

Iola   Right.

Iola *watches* **Mared** *for a bit.   Then –*

Iola   How did she say things, then?

Mared (*looks at her, then:*)   She just had one of those voices
That makes you laugh.

Iola   And did you laugh?

Mared   No.

Beat.

I told her to piss off, and go fuck herself.

Iola (*beat*)   OK.

Mared   There's –
– the handbook makes it very clear
You do not get to laugh at clientele
No matter what they say.
So I didn't dare even – titter.

Iola   You just told her to piss off –

Mared   And go fuck herself, yeah.

Iola (*beat*)   And what did your supervisor say?

Mared (*looks at her, then:*)   I couldn't hear.

Iola   Right.

Mared   'Cause he talks in this really really quiet little
voice all the time.

Beat.

And 'cause even as he was coming over I knew
I didn't wanna hear anything he had to say –

She hesitates. **Iola** *waits for her to continue.*

So I started to go 'fuck off fuck off fuck off' –
– in like a chant.
Just to make sure not one word he said would reach my
ears.

Iola   Mm.

Mared   And at the same time I looked out the window
To make sure I wouldn't
Pick up even a gist through watching his lips move.

Iola (*beat*)   See, I don't know what to say now.
I don't know if it's helping you, being here, keeping busy,
Keeping your mind off it / or

Mared   / And this bitch tells me
She's got this – and she actually
Uses the words – 'hot date' tonight,
And how's she gonna get ready for her hot date
Without hot water?
I say to her, OK, we'll do our best
To get an engineer out to you today.

Beat.

And I ask her for
Details of her boiler.
Details of her problem with her boiler.
Details of her gas account.
Details of her address.
And any other detail she feels might help us render best
service.

Beat.

She says: no.
She says, no, because she's already given her details
To someone in our office.
She's explained her problem and asked for our help
And now she's not calling to explain, nor ask:
She's calling to complain.

Beat.

I say to her, if you'd like to give me a name, I can transfer
you
To the customer adviser who's been advising you already
today –

Beat.

She says: no.
Tough luck.
You don't get rid of me as easy as that.

Beat.

I say, I'm not trying to get rid of you, madam.
I just want to save your precious time
By referring your complaint to someone
Who's familiar with your situation.

Iola   Mared . . .

Mared   And anyway she's forgotten the name of the pleb
She'd spoken to this morning:
It not being her job to remember names of people
Her having more important things in her life
Than the names of people.

Iola   – Mared –

Mared   I ask if she's been allocated an enquiry number
this morning.
Yes, she says.
I ask her if she wrote down her enquiry number,
She confirms she did write the number down,
What with her not being a total fucking idiot
I ask her what her enquiry number might be.

Iola   – listen to me, Mared –

Mared   But she can't give me the number,
Because she's written it on a notepad
Which lives on the table, next to the phone,
And now she's out clothes-shopping for her hot date
While the notepad is still at home
On its little fucking table.

Beat.

I say to her: have you considered
Once in your life

You could wash yourself in cold water, madam,
Like all our nans and grampies managed to do
In days gone by.
She says: no.
She can't wash herself in cold water
What with her not being an ignorant, semi-literate, mud-hut
dwelling / peasant.

Iola   / Mared.

Mared (*beat*)   In the background.
Over her phone.
I can hear
John Simpson, or
Some other fucker from the BBC.
She's in a bar,
There's all the noise of people in a bar
And the fucker from the BBC in some foreign desert
Repeating once again key lines,
Names, ranks and numbers killed.
These figures, of course, approximate,
And subject, of course, to reporting restrictions.
And the bitch on the phone telling me
She has more important things to be worrying about
Than the thermostat on her bloody boiler. I say to her:
I know how you feel, madam.

Iola (*beat*)   Perhaps you should take a few days off.

Mared   It was dead fucking funny.
I just can't explain quite –

Iola   They let you.

Mared   – I can't explain quite how or why.

Iola   They let you take a few days off.

At times like this.

Mared   You had to be there, I suppose.

Scene Nine

Outside.

Mared *is sitting on her own.*

Iola *appears. She's carrying a bottle of Lucozade.*
She sits next to **Mared***. Gives the Lucozade to her.*

Mared   Cheers.

Mared *takes a mouthful of Lucozade.*

Pauses for a second.

Iola   Is it coming back up?

Mared (*beat*)   I don't *think* –
– no, I'm fine.

Iola *produces a strip of painkillers from her pocket: passes them to*
Mared*.*

Mared   Thanks.

She pushes a couple of tablets through the strip: swallows them.

They sit for a while.

Iola   You did a tidy job on Susannah.

Mared   I thought so.

Iola   I've never seen anyone cry so much in public.

Mared   Hopefully she won't go wasting her money
On waterproof eyeliner any more
Because, as everyone saw:
It isn't waterproof at all.

Iola   And you knew what you were doing
With Manda and Kev.

Mared   Yeah; and it was dead hard work,
And it got me no thanks from you at all.
According to what I remember, anyway.

Iola (*beat*)   I do not –

Iola *stops herself.*

Then, quieter:

I do not fancy fucking Kev.

Mared   Yeah, but a nice meal,
Bottle of wine or three
Who knows where the evening might lead?

Iola   He's with someone else,
They're very happy together,
And you can just fuck off.

Mared *looks at her.*

Looks away.

Iola   Look, Mared –

Mared   I'm taking it, then, that everyone's totally pissed off with me.

Iola   Of course they're not.

Mared *looks at her.*

Iola   Well – they're not.
Sorry to disappoint.

Beat.

They get it, you know?

Mared   They get what?

Iola   You were pissed, for a start.

Beat.

And who wouldn't be a bit –

Beat.

Everyone's just wondering why you haven't been out of your head / since

Mared   / Who gives a fuck if he's with someone else?
Life's just that little bit too fucking short.

Iola   Too short for upsetting people, then?

Mared   You're starting to piss me off now.
Perhaps you should find
Someone else to chatter at.

Iola   D'you remember how you got home?

Mared   In a taxi.

Iola   After Kev told you you'd had enough,
You tried to hit him.
You failed.
You fell over.

Mared   Which would explain the state of my trousers . . .

Iola (*looks at her*)   We tried to help you up.
But you pushed us away.
You ran out of the club.
We came after you but
You'd just run off.
We lost you.
We spent three-quarters of an hour looking.
And when we came across you, finally.
You were with two men.
Men in suits.
Men in their forties, fifties more than likely.
One of the men had puke down his jacket.
Your puke, I took it, but I couldn't be absolutely sure.

Beat.

The other one – the one without puke down his jacket
He was kissing you.
And to be fair you were kissing him back.
He also was pushing his hand
Down the front of your jeans.
His friend
– the other man –

– the one *with* puke down his jacket –
Had opened the buttons of your shirt
He had pushed up your bra
And he was sucking
Your left tit.
I could hear him, slurping away.

Mared   And you are making this up.

Iola   I told you –
– I shouted at you,
At the men.
You started to walk towards me
The second bloke still hanging off your tit –

Mared   You are making this all up.

Iola   And you said to me.
You explained to me –

She stops.

I told the men I was phoning the police
They laughed, they wandered away.

Beat.

You watched them going and you turned
And you said to me
'Life is just that little bit too –'

Beat.

You can guess the rest.

Scene Ten

Outside.

Mared *is lying, quietly asleep.*
Iola *sits nearby, watching her.*

Iola   Mared.

Mared *sits up.*

Iola   You OK?

Mared *looks around her, blinking.*

Iola   You were talking in your sleep.

Mared   Was I?

Iola   Maybe shouting more than talking.

Mared   I've been asleep?

Iola   Yeah.
You all right?

Mared   I'm not –

Looks at **Iola***.*

Iola   What?

Mared   Nothing.

Iola *pulls a bar of chocolate from her pocket.*
Offers the chocolate to **Mared***.*
Mared *looks at the chocolate: at* **Iola***.*

Iola   You want some?

Mared   Yeah.

Mared *doesn't move.*

Iola   Go on, then.

Mared *takes some of the chocolate.*
She eats it.
Iola *scoffs the rest of the bar.*
Mared *looks in her pocket.*
She finds what she's looking for.
She pulls it out.
And it isn't what she's expecting.
It's a mobile bill.

Iola   What's that?

Mared   Mobile bill.

Iola   Is it –

Mared   – a nightmare?

Iola   Mm.

Mared   Yeah.

Iola   I told you you should call your brother from the office.

Mared   Yeah.

Iola   It's a total rip-off phoning abroad off your mobile
It shouldn't be much more than calling from a landline really,
I mean, yeah, the call starts off on the mobile
But as soon as it goes into the system and up to the satellite
It's exactly the same as calling from an ordinary phone so:
How come the extra eight quid a minute?

Mared   Oh my God.

Iola   Well, yeah.

Mared   Oh my fucking God.

Iola   There's nothing . . . wrong, is there?

Mared   I'm not sure. I mean I hope not.
I mean: is there? Anything wrong,
With me?

Iola   There's the pitiful state of your hair.
The mess you call a personal life.
Your – what shall I say – less than positive attitude towards
the world, and all the people and things which live in it.

Mared   But nothing else?

Iola   No.

Mared   Nothing . . . to do with my family?

Iola   Apart from that they all hate you

And want you to fail as a daughter and a person.
Or so you / claim

Iola's *speech is cut off by* **Mared** *grabbing her and giving her a massive hug.*

Mared   Oh my God.
Oh my fucking God.
Thank fuck for that.

Iola *pushes her away.*

Iola   Piss off!
I want the real Mared back, please.

Mared   Sorry. It's just –
– the sunshine.

Iola   Yes, it's very nice, if you like premature ageing.

Mared   And look at the skaters –
They fall, they hurt themselves,
And they jump straight up.

They watch the skaters for a moment.

Mared   OK, obviously, they don't always
Jump straight up.
Occasionally there is a certain amount
Of screaming and crying but –
They're – fearless.

Iola   They're senseless.

Mared   Look at the way their eyes are shining . . .

Iola   I think that's 'cause they're all on speed, Mar.

Mared   It's not 'cause they're on speed.
Their eyes are shining and
Their cheeks are rosy red and
Their voices are clear and bright because
They're just getting off on life.

Iola   Mared . . .

Mared   On running, and jumping, and crashing into the pavement.

Iola   You're going to get yourself in so much trouble Talking like that.

Mared   The speed just helps them stay up nights.

Iola   For fuck's sake!

Mared (*turns to her*)   What?

Iola   Look. I don't mind you talking like that. 'Cause I'm a friend to you.

Mared   Talking like what?

Iola (*beat*)   We can just forget about this now, if you want.

Mared   Talking like what?

Iola (*beat*)   Talking in that Lewis-Carrollian-Jabberwockyesque-guttural-nonsense language.

Mared   What d'you mean – guttural nonsense language?

Beat.

I was speaking Welsh.

Iola   Welsh.

Mared   Yeah.

Iola   You were speaking – the language 'Welsh'?

Mared   As you are now.

Iola *looks away.*

Mared   What?

Iola   You're just being stupid now.

Mared   What language are you speaking then, Iola?

Beat

Iola?

Iola   The handbook makes it very clear
You do not get to ask linguistic questions of Iola
No matter what she says.

Mared (*beat*)   What language are you speaking, Iola?

Iola   Don't push it, Mar.

Mared   No.

Iola   Think, Mared. Think why we can't be speaking
The language 'Welsh'. Just don't think about it
Too much.

Silence.

We'll just stop, then.
We'll just stop this conversation right now
And go into the office and carry on with
Whatever it is we do there
And when we come out
The kids' eyes will still be shining
And not just because they're all on speed, and
Their voices will still be lifted with joy and
We, the Welsh people, will still bestride the world
Like fuckin cultural colossi.

Iola *waits for* **Mared** *to react.*
Mared *says nothing.*
Iola *starts to get up.*

Iola   Fine.

She walks off.
Mared *stays where she is.*
Iola *comes back.*

Iola   Mared.

Mared   What language are we speaking, then?

Iola   Please don't.

Mared   Iola.

Iola   I don't know what language you think we're jabbering on in
But – we can't be speaking the language 'Welsh'
Because the last person to speak the language 'Welsh' died
In the year sixteen hundred and seventy-five.

Mared (*beat*) ⌣Oh shit.

Iola   You know what's going to happen now, don't you.

Mared *says nothing.*

Iola   Don't you, Mared?

Mared   I'm going to wake up.

Iola   Mm.

Mared   When I do wake up: how much
Will have been a dream?
All of it, or –
– just this bit now,
When he's been still alive?

Iola   Mared. I'm sorry.
I tried my best.
But you won't be fucking told, will you.

Scene Eleven

Inside.

Mared *is alone, slumped over her desk.*
A tone sounds in her headset.
She sits up with a start.

Mared   Yes. I'm here, Christ . . .
Sorry, I meant – good morning, Mared speaking
How can I help you?
That's fine, the change of address has gone through.
While you're on the line, madam, can I interest you
In a Gasguard health check for your new property?
No? Right.

Thanks so much.

The tone sounds again, announcing a new call.

Hello, Mared speaking.
Yes. Yeah. No, I'm afraid that really isn't my fault, sir.
Because we're not responsible for your electricity supply.
We do your gas.
I can give your their number, yes,
But I can't put you through.
Well, because they're an entirely different company.

Beat.

I don't supposed you'd be interested in having
Your gas appliances checked at all?
Fair enough, sir.
Bye.

The tone.

Hello, Mared speaking, how can I –
Yes. I can set that up for you right now.
No problem.
And – while you're on the line, madam –
OK. Bye then.

The tone again.

Hello, Mared speaking.
Not tonight, no, but someone could be with you
First thing tomorrow.
I realise it must be very inconvenient for you, sir.
Mm. Yeah.
We do recommend all our customers give their gas
appliances
An annual Gasguard health check, precisely to prevent
These situations cropping up.
No, I know that's not much help to you now, sir.
Yes, I will give you my team leader's name.
I know.
I do realise that.

Well, I'll tell you what.
What if I give you a car. Would that help?
Seriously, I've got one going spare, and –
I don't drive myself.
No, it's not stolen.
It's – I've inherited it.

Beat.

Well it's blue.
I can't really tell you beyond that, I'm not much of
An automotive enthusiast, but –

She stops.

Pushes a button on her keyboard to cut the call. Takes off her headset.

Collects herself for a moment.

Then replaces her headset, pushes another button on her keyboard.

The tone announces another call.

Hello, Mared speaking, how can I –
No, I'm not in India. I'm in Wales.
Yes I'm sure that pretty much is
The same thing as far as you're concerned.
Now would you mind telling me
How exactly I can help you, sir?

Scene Twelve

Outside.

Mared *and* **Iola** *are sitting.*

Mared   It's all still here. It doesn't go away.

Mared *searches in her pocket.*
She finds what she's looking for.
It is what she's dreading.
She pulls out the black card.

Iola What's that?

Mared Funeral invite.

Iola Oh.

Beat.

D'you want me to come with you?

Mared It'll be free booze.
Middle-aged men.
That's your sort of party, isn't it?

Iola You could just say, yes
I want you to come, Iola.
If in fact you do.

Silence.

Mared I'm lost for words.
I'm lost for everything else as well.

They sit.

I catch myself on the edge of saying things like
'This can't be real.'
Imagine.

Silence.

I said to him:
You're too much of a wimp to go in the army.
He said: it's all right for you,
You live such a dreamlife anyway
But I . . . want to do something.

Beat.

What's that supposed to mean, I said.
Bombing peasants in the Third World?
That's doing something, is it?

Beat.

I just wanna do something.

He actually said that.
How fucking kitsch can you get?

Beat.

I said to him:
You're too much of a wimp to go in the army,
You'll get yourself fucking killed.
And I actually fucking said that.
I said: you'll get yourself fucking killed.
Twat.

They sit.

He's done something now.
He's done something to me. Amongst others.

Beat.

You've never done anything in your life, have you?

Iola *shakes her head.*

Mared   No-one's done anything to you?

Iola *gets up.*
She goes over to her desk. **Mared** *watches her.*
From under her desk **Iola** *pulls a great big box, in ribbons and exciting wrapping paper.*

Mared   Oh fuck . . .

Iola *comes back to sit with* **Mared**.
She opens the big box.
Inside, she finds a smaller box, in even more exciting wrapping paper.
She opens the smaller box, and finds a golden envelope.

Iola *looks at* **Mared**.
And then tears open the golden envelope, and finds –
– a folded piece of paper.

She reads, and summarises.

Iola   Two marriages. Three children.
Cancer scare in my mid-fifties.

I make a full recovery, then
Finally pop it at
The grand old age of seventy-nine.

Mared   How?

Iola   Car crash. After my second husband
Falls asleep at the wheel.

Mared   So . . . you go together.

Iola   Yeah.

Mared   Nice.

Beat.

Lucky bitch.

Iola   Mared . . .

Mared   They're flying his body back tonight.
I don't know, do they deliver it to us
Or do we go to the air base to collect it,
Or what.

Beat.

Can you do something for me?

Iola   What?

Mared   Anything.
Anything at all.
I don't know.

Iola *looks away.*
They sit.

Mared   You might as well go in, then.
If you can't do anything to help.

Iola *sits.*
She takes the folded sheet of paper.
She takes a pair of scissors from the box.

She folds the paper, and cuts it, and cuts it again, and makes a pattern
of people holding hands with each other.
She shows the paper people to **Mared**.

Mared   That's shit.

Beat.

You may as well go in,
Or you'll freeze.

Iola *gets out her pack of fags.*
From the pack of fags, she takes a lighter.
She lights the flame.
Adjusts the lighter so it's on the highest setting.
Shuffles closer to **Mared** *so they can share the heat from the flame.*

Mared   You might as well go in,
Or you'll starve.

Iola *pulls out her chocolate: offers it to* **Mared**.

Mared   You might as well go in,
Or you'll get in trouble with Kev.

Iola   I don't think so.

Mared   What're you gonna do, then?
Just sit here with me?

Iola   Yeah.

Mared (*beat*)   But you'll go in in the end.

Iola *says nothing.*

Mared   You will.

Iola *says nothing.*

Mared   I know what you're like.

They sit.
And gradually, the day turns to night.

They sit.
And gradually, the summer turns to winter.

They sit.
And gradually, the city disappears beneath grass and wild flowers.

They sit.
And gradually, the buildings all crumble to the ground.

Mared (*looks up*)   I think I'm gonna go in now.

Iola   I'll come with you.

Printed in Great Britain
by Amazon